THE
HIRE TACTICS™

The Four Milestones for Finding Civilian Employment

Tom Stein, USMC Retired
Greg Wood, CCMP

Adapted from the four books in TheHireTactics™ Job Search Series

www.TheHireTactics.com

PETERSON'S

THE HIRE TACTICS™

The Four Milestones for Finding Civilian Employment

by Tom Stein, USMC Retired and Greg Wood, CCMP

About Peterson's

Peterson's provides the accurate, dependable, high-quality education content and guidance you need to succeed. No matter where you are on your academic or professional path, you can rely on Peterson's print and digital publications for the most up-to-date education exploration data, expert test-prep tools, and top-notch career success resources—everything you need to achieve your goals.

For more information, contact Peterson's, 3 Columbia Circle, Suite 205, Albany, NY 12203-5158; 800-338-3282 Ext. 54229; or find us online at www.petersonsbooks.com.

Bernadette Webster, Managing Editor; Jill C. Schwartz, Editor; Ray Golaszewski, Publishing Operations Manager; Linda M. Williams, Composition Manager

ISBN-13: 978-0-7689-3782-4

Tom Stein, Lt. Col. USMC Retired
GreyHawk Enterprises
8502 E. Chapman Avenue, Suite #157
Orange, CA 92869

A Service-Disabled Veteran-Owned Small Business
(SDVOSB) CAGE/NCAGE: 6KBY4

Printed in the United States of America

10 9 8 7 6 5 4 3 2 1 15 14 13

Disclosures and Disclaimers

Sorry but no one—including the authors and publisher—can guarantee you a job or any particular job. Your success will depend on numerous factors outside our control including, but not limited to, your effort, experience, education, location, and match to an employer's needs.

While care and diligence have been taken in preparing the information contained in these books, neither the authors nor the publisher guarantees its accuracy. It is sold and used by the reader with the understanding that the authors, contributors, publisher, and sales outlets are not engaged in rendering legal, financial, or other professional advice. The reader is provided with guidelines, strategies, and ideas that may or may not be applicable or appropriate for the reader's situation.

Laws and practices vary from state to state and if financial, legal, or other technical expertise or assistance is required, the services of an experienced and competent professional should be sought. The author, contributors, and publisher specifically disclaim any liability that is incurred from the use or application of the contents of this book and system.

This book and the related materials are adapted from TheHireRoad™ system developed by the author, Greg Wood, CCMP, and proven in over 12 years of use by individuals, small businesses, corporations, and trainers worldwide.

In addition to this combined volume, TheHireTactics™ is available as four individual ebooks, each focused on just one of the four milestones specifically for military veterans looking for civilian employment.

This book is a combination of four best-selling books which are dedicated to helping military veterans succeed in their job search mission. The four different sections of this book are designed to be short and sweet so veterans can quickly begin using this proven job search approach. All four books are available as ebooks.

Section 1—VETERAN EMPLOYMENT TACTICS—Packaging Yourself for Job Hunting Success

The first section in TheHireTactics™ series introduces military veterans to the tools you need to brand yourself to ensure you, the military veteran, separate yourself from your competition. In this section, you will learn how the job search system really works and how to use your tactical advantage as a military veteran!

Section 2—FIRE YOUR RESUME!—Military Edition

The second section in TheHireTactics™ series is one of our most popular. In it veterans will learn how to avoid turning a job search into C.R.A.P. (Clicking, Reviewing, Applying, and Praying). Learn why it is mission critical to get the intel and package it so you can successfully penetrate the hidden job market. Learn how to educate employers about the value of your service and values you bring as a military veteran!

Section 3—LOCK AND LOAD!—24 Job Interview Questions Military Veterans Need to Know!

Being asked for an interview means you are 80 percent of the way to accomplishing your mission. The interview is where you seal the deal and preparation is the key to success! In the third section in TheHireTactics™ series you'll learn how to demonstrate the value you bring to the table by conducting a tactical and strategic interview that will greatly enhance your chances of winning the job offer. Additional questions pertinent to all job interviews can be found in Greg Wood's book, *Nailed It!*

Section 4—PAY DAY!—Negotiating Your True Worth, Not Just a Salary

Let's face it, you as a military veteran are probably not used to negotiating your pay. A table from the Pentagon listing your rank and time in service pretty much sets your paycheck and benefits. In this fourth section in TheHireTactics™ series, you'll learn how to evaluate whether a job is worth taking and then, if it is, how to negotiate the difference between what you're offered and your true worth to the organization.

ABOUT THE AUTHORS

Tom Stein, USMC Retired

Tom Stein is a business owner, experienced senior executive, author, and public speaker. Prior to working in Corporate America, he was a Lieutenant Colonel in the United States Marine Corps specializing in Aviation, Information Technology, Logistics, Operational Threat Analysis, Contingency Planning, and Education. Tom is a graduate of the United States Naval Academy and holds numerous degrees and certificates in Aviation, Information Technology, and Education. As an executive program manger he has held executive positions and designations in his fields of expertise and has worked with Fortune 500 companies like Apple, Dell, Ingram Micro, and WalMart.

Never losing his touch with his military roots, Tom continues his passion for aviation as an Adjunct Professor and Mentor for Embry-Riddle Aeronautical University, where as a faculty and staff member since 1988, he instructs and develops programs for undergraduate and graduate students.

As a Certified Career Management Professional (CCMP) Tom teaches classes nationwide to assist vererans in their transition from military to civilian careers. He is also a Board Member and former Chairman of the Board of the Orange County Veteran Employment Committee.

Tom Stein
TheHireTactics™
8502 E. Chapman Avenue, Suite #157
Orange, CA 92869
Office: (714) 356-2239
E-mail: Tom@TheHireTactics.com

A Service-Disabled Veteran-Owned Small Business (SDVOSB)
CAGE/NCAGE: 6KBY4

Greg Wood, CCMP

Greg Wood is a Certified Career Management Professional (CCMP) who has experienced firsthand the challenges and anxiety of being unemployed several times during his 30-plus years of business experience. With more than 13 years of experience in both outplacement and executive search, Greg earned his reputation as a preeminent career counselor through the creation of TheHireRoad, an innovative, strategic approach to the job search. His unique program takes job seekers step-by-step through the entire job-search process, providing all the resources and tools necessary to achieve differentiation and shorten their time in transition at a very critical time in their lives.

An excellent trainer and presenter, Mr. Wood is a frequent guest speaker at a variety of professional and career transition support groups around the nation. In 2010, he was interviewed by talk show host Bill Handel on KFI AM640 radio in Los Angeles, one of the top news/talk shows in the country. Greg has also appeared on the "Job Seekers Clinic Show" on KFWB News Talk 980.

Greg's corporate background includes domestic and international experience in a variety of industries including executive search, publishing, high technology, and health care. He has held senior management positions with mid-size as well as major Fortune 500 corporations.

To contact Greg for keynotes, corporate outplacement, and one-on-one consultation:

Greg Wood
TheHireChallenge
4340 E. Indian School Road, Suite 21
Phoenix, AZ 85018
Office: (602) 237-5366
E-mail: Greg@TheHireChallenge.com

For more information on TheHireRoad™ Job Search System:
http://www.TheHireChallenge.com

TESTIMONIALS

Here are just a few comments from job seekers who have taken TheHireRoad™ approach:

"I think TheHireRoad program should become part of the workforce development system as an added feature available in the One Stop Career Centers throughout the United States. I highly recommend this product."

Jim McShane
Public Administrator, Illinois (WIA)
Workforce Investment Act System

"I had the pleasure of meeting Greg about a month ago and learning about the job search strategies he teaches with TheHireRoad. In the space of those four weeks I have been actively applying TheHireRoad resources and strategy for communicating added value to potential employers. In that short time I received three invitations for interviews with hiring managers of companies I was most interested in!

This week I was offered a position at one of these companies which I gratefully accepted. Although the outcome speaks for itself, it was the process of getting there with Greg's help for which I am most THANKFUL. I appreciate that Greg not only gave me the resources, but he helped me to use them with the most impact. I am humbled and grateful for within four weeks of being suddenly unemployed, I have what looks like will be a great job."

Ron Sato
Santa Ana, California

"TheHireRoad™ was pivotal in my search for new employment, giving me all the professional tools necessary to maximize my employment search, prepare for interviews and create a post-interview presentation of myself, all of which enabled me to stand out from the competition and land the perfect job. I would recommend Greg and TheHireRoad™ to anyone who is looking to put all the integral pieces of a new employment search together."

Leslie Rush
Oceanside, California

"Greg is an excellent teacher and an inspirational role model. He is empowering while sharing his knowledge and motivates job seekers to test his unique techniques in real life. Greg has been a great supporter throughout the process, providing practical advice and hope. I highly recommend Greg's services to all on the road to success."

Klara Detrano
Costa Mesa, California

"TheHireRoad was very effective and helped shorten my time between jobs. The seminar is a welcome change from the standard advice found in numerous books and tapes, especially the approach to interviewing. I'm sure the strategies will be just as valuable if and when I find myself in transition again."

Larry Weimann
St. Louis, Missouri

"TheHireRoad has led to spectacular results. I have used the techniques provided on the CDs and achieved results that I could never have gotten using other methods. The recommendations in TheHireRoad definitely got me noticed and helped me feel more confident in my interviews. Thank you for providing this very helpful job search tool."

Robert Lee
Simi Valley, California

"I did use TheHireRoad program. The CDs and the DVD were great. I have had three job offers, accepted one last week, and started Monday."

Jason Stone
Alpharetta, Georgia

"TheHireRoad really gave me the help I needed. I went into the interview with a lot of confidence and got the offer!"

Susan Cole
Indianapolis, Indiana

"TheHireRoad was an instrumental part of beginning my job search. The in-home seminar turned the anxiety of the interview into a position of knowledge and confidence. I am very happy to have made the choice to go with TheHireRoad and I have nothing but praise for their techniques, knowledge, and strategies."

Robert King
Whittier, California

"The techniques I learned with this program have helped me revitalize my job search and boost my confidence. Now I'm actually getting interviews!"

Donna Schowalter
Newport Beach, California

For more information visit: http://www.TheHireChallenge.com.

CONTENTS

APPENDIX

SECTION 1

Veteran Employment Tactics

INTRODUCTION

Welcome to the New Job Reality

Welcome to TheHireTactics™—our series presenting job search strategies and tactics for military veterans.

I'm Tom Stein, retired Lt. Col. USMC, and the proud coauthor of this book. This book is not for the weak-minded nor those without heart. You have served your country well and now you have a new challenge. This trial is nothing like boot camp, but it is still a challenge that will require the skills and talents you mastered in the military. As you read on, you will quickly see how these new tools will help you master this new obstacle that you face.

The contents of this book are based on the highly successful job search system, TheHireRoad™, created by my friend and coauthor, Greg Wood, CCMP. He has the technical skills and I have the direct experience with transitioning from the military to the civilian workforce. I used Greg's system in my own job search so I speak from personal experience!

As you read, we will share how to develop and use a proven strategic approach for your job search instead of the traditional resume-based approach. Using this new approach and its tools will help shorten your job transition time.

The content in TheHireTactics™ series does not remotely resemble any of the information found in those self-help "for dummies," series. This book is not "A Complete Idiot's Guide," to job searching and does not contain easy-to-do tasks designed to get you a job in four easy steps or just "24 days." We make no such promises. This series is for job seekers who are frustrated, discouraged, and increasingly fed up and want answers and solutions; not clever book titles and unrealistic promises.

WHY TheHireTactics™

Some of you are coming straight out of the military from your initial commitment and some of you are departing the military after a very successful career. It does not matter who you are or where you served in the military, because 99 percent of the population has never served in the military.

But within that 99 percent are employers who do have problems to solve. They hire people who can **solve** those problems. Sound familiar? They have a mission to carry out and they need people to implement the strategies and use the tactics needed to solve the problem and win the day.

The employers have problems and they are looking for someone to help them. The goal is to make sure they see **you**, and convince them you're the right fit!

YOU MUST BE SEEN BY THE EMPLOYER AS THAT SOLUTION!

Several times in my life I have been faced with the challenge of finding new employment. I admit it, sometimes it was because I wanted to start a different career or I became bored. You might find yourself in the same situation.

While in the military you usually have a new boss every six to eighteen months. Also, you are on the move going to training, to a career-level school, or moving to a new duty station. At least I did, and that was one of the great things about the military that I enjoyed. Always a new goal, new surroundings, or new adventure. In the first fifteen years of my career I moved eight times.

In corporate America there is also a constant change of management and sometimes it's not for the better. But unlike the military, many employees hunker down and refuse to move and wait until they are RIF'd (reduction in force). In this alien environment, I've experienced frustration at times and when I decided to move on there was very little support and essentially no road map to guide me.

I was struggling and soon realized there were a lot of other people just like me who needed help. And when I discovered the amount of funds being wasted on ineffective programs and unemployment benefits I decide to get more involved with translating Greg Wood's TheHireRoad™ Job Search System into the road map my fellow veterans needed. It became my mission to meet the need!

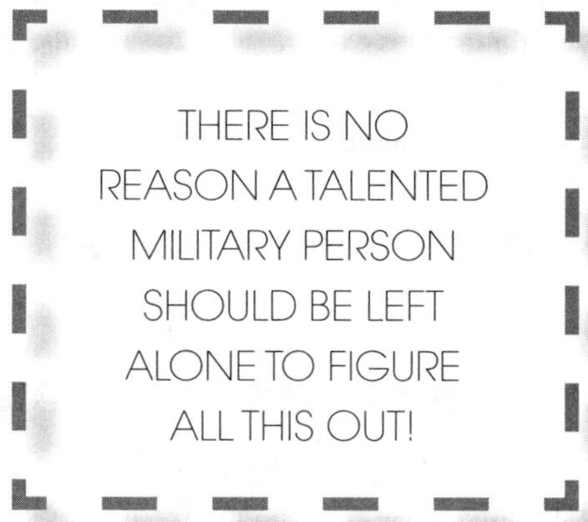

It's why I became more involved with military affairs and transition programs and co-created TheHireTactics™ Veterans Job Search System. My passion is helping the military, and as a successful businessman and an adjunct professor for a major university for the past fifteen years, I've successfully counseled hundreds of military personnel facing the challenges of a job search. While there are many sources of job search information, many focus on outdated, traditional approaches that no longer work.

For example, look at the career section of any Sunday newspaper or read job search tips online. Notice the use of the same old techniques and advice that have been around for decades. You won't find anything new! You can pull a newspaper from the 1980s, 1990s or early 2000s and find the exact same information about resumes, cover letters, and wearing a nice suit.

YOU NEED NEW TOOLS AND NEW TACTICS FOR THIS NEW JOB REALITY.

Things have changed. Times have changed. Times are tough. And the military is constantly resizing.

Job search success in our new economy requires creativity, a willingness to think outside the box, and innovative approaches to meet the challenges of finding employment.

Are you willing to change your mindset to succeed in today's fiercely competitive job market?

Are you willing to learn new techniques for the new job reality?

If so, read on!

THE FOUR MILESTONES

When creating TheHireRoad™ Greg focused on what it took to communicate successfully with potential employers. After hundreds of interviews with job seekers and a decade of working inside both large corporations and small businesses as a consultant, he discovered there are **Four Milestones to an effective job search in the civilian arena:**

MILESTONE 1—Packaging: This milestone is all about using innovative marketing tools that clearly differentiate you from your competition. We want to ensure you can show potential employers how your military experience translates into real value. This is the focus of **SECTION 1** *Veteran Employment Tactics* in this book.

MILESTONE 2—Promotion: To get a job you need to educate the business community (hiring managers) by broadcasting your value as a military veteran, NOT your resume. This is the focus of **SECTION 2** *Fire Your Resume!* We discuss the innovative tools that job seekers need today to be successful in getting past human resources and in front of a hiring manager.

MILESTONE 3—Product Demonstration: The interview is the crux of your job search. To be successful and become the candidate of choice, you need to conduct a strategic interview versus a traditional interview. You need to be able to explain to the hiring manager why your military experience makes you a better candidate. This is the subject of **SECTION 3** *Lock and Load!* that provides 24 critical questions often asked in job interviews and suggested answers to those questions.

MILESTONE 4—Pricing: One of the most difficult challenges for job seekers is determining a fair offer for employment. We in the military know what everyone makes; it's public knowledge. The funny part is you always wondered why the hell a lieutenant got paid so much. The answer: college, but I digress. Milestone 4 is where you'll negotiate the difference between what you're offered and your true worth to the organization. Transitioning military have to be very careful to understand the range of income. There is a difference between what you need to survive and what you deserve or want. Military veterans can be taken advantage of because they lack knowledge and experience in how salaries are set, and what bonuses should be offered. This is discussed in **SECTION 4** *Pay Day!* in this book.

So let's get started with MILESTONE 1—Packaging. You will learn more about the process and the marketing tools you'll need to clearly distinguish yourself so you can achieve job search success!

CHAPTER ONE

Differentiation is Critical

The main goal of the four milestones is to help you achieve **differentiation**. Differentiation is critical to ensure you stand out from the herd of other job applicants. If you do not standout or if you're not the outstanding or preferred candidate, you are simply another commodity applicant.

One definition of commodity is:

A PRODUCT, SUCH AS FOOD, GRAINS, OR METALS, WHICH IS INTERCHANGEABLE WITH ANOTHER PRODUCT OF THE SAME TYPE. THE PRICE OF THE COMMODITY IS SUBJECT TO SUPPLY AND DEMAND.

Notice the key words **interchangeable** and **supply and demand**. If you do not differentiate yourself then you are interchangeable with every other candidate. In today's economy, there are far more job seekers than jobs. Depending on the job expertise required, there may be 100 to more than 5,000 applicants for a single job.

This means the supply of interchangeable job applicants greatly exceeds the jobs available. Under the law of supply and demand, when there is a lot of a commodity, the price (salary) falls.

So you do NOT want to be a commodity. You want to **stand out** from all other applicants and be perceived as the **outstanding** candidate. You want to be the one hired and for a value that is worthy of your experience and expertise.

Your goal is the word used at the start of this chapter—DIFFERENTIATION. In other words, how do you distinguish yourself from all other candidates? How do you separate yourself from all those people chasing the same jobs that you are pursuing?

GOOD NEWS #1—You are already different because of your military background. In addition, you have achieved one of the most difficult transitions anyone can make: the civilian to military transition.

GOOD NEWS #2—Virtually all job seekers follow the traditional approach to a job search that relies on want ads and Internet job boards. Desperate job seekers have been led to mistakenly believe that a powerful resume and a knock-'em-dead cover letter will get them in the door for an interview and in front of the hiring manager. However, this approach fails miserably. You will NOT be using those tactics!

C.R.A.P.

What many in the job search industry refer to as the traditional approach we call C.R.A.P.: **C**licking, **R**eviewing, **A**pplying, and **P**raying.

Millions of job applicants just like you spend their days clicking around the Internet on job boards, Craigslist, corporate websites, and maybe even reading the old-fashioned newspaper want ads. You review the descriptions and decide that maybe you are close enough for the position and decide to apply.

If you are an experienced job seeker, you may take a moment to customize your resume and cover letter to more closely match the job description. But eventually you will submit the same old resume that everyone else submits and pray the phone rings to set up an interview.

Sound familiar?

Have you done the same series of actions day in and day out?

If you have, I can guarantee you are getting the same result as all the other veterans and job seekers we counsel: **Nothing**.

You are simply adding your paperwork to a massive pile of identical resumes. And that assumes you get past the automated "meatgrinder" resume-scanning software that searches out special keywords and phrases that may or may not be on your resume.

We all know there has to be a better way.

When I was in your position, I knew I had a lot to offer an employer in terms of skills, experience, and expertise as a retired officer from the Marine Corps. But I needed to get noticed. I had to somehow stand out during every step of the job search process. I needed differentiation.

And so do you!

You need to determine how you are going to stand out to the employers with jobs you can do. And you do that in two steps: selling yourself and defining your value.

STEP 1—SELLING YOURSELF

The first step for job search success is to get comfortable with the idea of selling yourself (ouch!).

You MUST understand that you are seen by potential employers as one product among many (thousands upon thousands) in the job market. Success in your job search will mean convincing prospective employers to buy you instead of the other products (job applicants). You need to become the one who solves their problem and meets their needs.

As you know, promotion in the military is based primarily on the achievement of certain skill levels and time spent in the service. You really don't have a lot of selling to do—you meet requirements and the paperwork is filed for more rank. Now you have to sell yourself as **THE** answer to why the employer was looking to hire someone. After all, you know this product better than anyone else in the world. You know your own strengths and weaknesses, likes and dislikes, and what you can and cannot do.

You need to take this information and create a winning sales pitch. In marketing terminology, this is called your Unique Selling Proposition or USP. A good USP will answer the questions in the mind of every interviewer you'll meet in the job-search process, which are:

- Why should I hire you?
- What makes you special?
- Why are you the best possible candidate for that job or that company?

Here are some examples of USP's:

- Through my proven and unique experience as a veteran, I use teamwork, initiative, dedication, adaptability, and my exceptional work ethic to help companies achieve greater profitability.
- With my unique experience as a veteran, I possess discipline, reliability, independent thinking, and a willingness to accept tasks and see them through to completion.
- As an experienced veteran I'm accustomed to being challenged, thinking quickly on my feet, demonstrating initiative, and striving to accomplish a task the first time. These are just some of the qualities that enable me to be a valuable contributor from day one of employment.

By the way, I have seen this step done so well by some job seekers that the hiring manager changed the job description to fit them instead of being measured against the original description! I have also seen applicants who were so well positioned that they created a job where one did not exist.

If you are not comfortable selling yourself, **Get over it**!

Let me give you an example of how presenting a great USP worked for me. When I decided to start a new career search I was very comfortable engaging with new opportunities. I knew *TheHireTactics* from front to back and my confidence was high.

There was an opportunity to be a vice president of a local trade school. It seemed perfect for me. In addition to my full-time job, I was teaching part-time during evenings and weekends as an adjunct professor and loved it. Many of my students were veterans and active duty personnel. So I put my "attack plan" together and investigated the college thoroughly. I contacted the college to inquire who the current president was.

I sent my biography, not a resume, and a nice letter of inquiry that explained that I would like to chat about the educational field and trade schools. I did not mention the position. Within two days, I received a call from the college president and he said he'd be very happy to have a chat and discuss the college trade school environment.

I was testing the waters and exploring to see if I would be a good fit for the organization. The president knew this. Remember, you are interviewing them as much as you are being interviewed. **It is always about value and fit.**

Our talk turned into a four-hour chat with lunch, tours, and introductions. He brought the VP position to my attention and asked for a resume. Within 24 hours I had put the resume together and sent it to him. A day later, I received a request to come back in for another chat. I quickly found out that the man I met, James, was not the campus president. He was the regional vice president and filling in until he could fill the two new vacancies, the vice president and president positions. The open president position was not public knowledge at the time of my visit.

After more interviews, James told me he felt I was presidential material and said he wanted to pursue hiring me as a president, not a vice president.

"Holy smokes," I thought. "The president of a college, you've got to be kidding me!"

So after six more interviews with senior executives, I was placed into a phenomenal training program for campus presidents. And all the while I had just been focused on being a VP. They not only saw my value, but also my potential. Had it not been for the *TheHireTactics*, I truly believe I would not have been given the opportunity.

You need to be comfortable with who you are and what you can do to help the future employer. You need to be confident that you can learn to do the job required. As a military veteran you have already faced more difficult challenges. You were prepared to literally give your life in the service of this country. You may think this is bragging but it isn't. You have incredible added value for any potential employer.

In **SECTION 3** *Lock and Load!* there are 24 questions that you will likely be asked in an interview. This inside look at interview questions is specially designed to help you showcase your military experience as well as your civilian potential. Being familiar with those questions and rehearsing with a coach may be something you need to consider if selling yourself is a terrifying thought.

STEP 2—DEFINING YOUR VALUE

I know this may shock many readers but . . .

Employers do NOT want to hire employees!

Employees are expensive and in today's economy can become a liability and not an asset. So employers hire only when they must. They hire to solve problems and provide the services they need. By hiring you, the company is investing in your ability to address issues and solve problems that will lead to greater profitability. In other words, your value will far outweigh the cost to employ you.

So when you create your USP, think of it as a commercial that will define your **value to the business community and to the company that is hiring.** Your USP will explain why they need to "buy" you and your skills, and it will give employers a reason to see you as an asset. You have to make sure they understand that you can solve their problems.

I cannot emphasize this enough!

Whether you're just beginning your job search or have been actively looking for some time, you must stop and determine your value before moving forward. If you cannot convince potential employers you are the answer to their needs, you do not stand much of a chance of being hired.

You need to have a good understanding of your professional value before you can begin to broadcast it to others. If you don't know the value you can bring to an organization, you have no business interviewing with that organization. Period.

I cannot tell you how many veteran job seekers I talk to who have no idea what they can do for an employer! They can recite all their experience, but they rarely can turn that into a clear statement of their value and why an employer would want to buy their skills. Telling me you want the job being advertised is not a compelling reason for me to hire you.

Often when I coach transitioning veterans they get frustrated trying to interpret their experience for the civilian world. "I was just a grunt!" That's their battle cry.

When I hear that statement it makes it sound like being "just a grunt" has no value. This is so far from the truth. Translated into corporate America speak, a grunt is someone who is extremely dedicated to a mission and that no matter how bad the situation is, or is going to be, sees the task completed. This is why companies like FedEx, UPS, Cintas, Toyota, and Wal-Mart target veterans. Such companies know they can usually rely on the veteran. They know that even on Christmas Eve that package or promise will be delivered and the veteran will not succumb to the pressure. **You see things through to the end. That is your value** (besides many other worthwhile attributes). The list is endless so focus on what value you can add. You will see this theme throughout this book.

Because of the present business climate, most associates are petrified to stand up, take charge, and see things through to the end. Service people and veterans are mostly problem solvers. We like a challenge, being part of a team that gets things done, and we enjoy a great sense of accomplishment. So be proud you were a grunt! That's a unique selling proposition.

IF YOU CANNOT CONVINCE A POTENTIAL EMPLOYER YOU ARE THE ANSWER TO THEIR NEEDS, YOU DO NOT STAND MUCH OF A CHANCE OF BEING HIRED!

So how do you determine your value?

To repeat, employers want employees to solve problems. So your value lies in how you can solve each potential employer's problems.

Your value comes from the blend of your SKILLS, EXPERIENCE, EXPERTISE, and STYLE. This is what you bring to the potential employer. Every tool you use, every strategy you implement, and every technique you incorporate in your job search must reflect your value.

SKILLS

Skills are the things you know how to do. Your skills are typically made up of soft skills and hard skills. Soft skills are readily transferable whereas hard skills are typically learned and may or may not transfer from one company to the next.

Soft skills are things like leadership, self-confidence, time management, problem solving, or positive attitude. These are skills that can be used virtually anywhere. They tend to be generic organizational and interpersonal skills. If you can supervise teams of office personnel or engineers, you're demonstrating soft skills that are easily transferable to a new employer. Military veterans often underestimate their soft skills in leadership and teamwork.

Hard skills are usually the processes used by a specific industry or company. You may be an expert in weapon deployments like unmanned aerial vehicles (UAVs), but if the new job you are seeking does not involve weapons, it is not a transferable skill. Similarly, you may know the building codes for Tulsa but not Los Angeles.

EXPERIENCE VERSUS EXPERTISE

Your EXPERIENCE includes the accomplishments or highlights from time spent in a particular job and industry, whereas your EXPERTISE characterizes your specialized skill set. For example, two civil engineers may have the same experience of being in the military for five years, but one has expertise in water infrastructure while the other is an expert in dams. Military lawyers may both work for JAG, but one may be an expert in contract law and the other in enemy combatants.

So, experience is your job **history**—your branch and rank. It is where you have worked and the positions you have held. By comparison, expertise is the specialized **skill set** you carry with you that can be applied to new problems with new employers.

For example, you may have experience as a Marine or a soldier, but your expertise is "aircraft engine mechanic" or "military police" or "public affairs photographer."

STYLE

Finally, your **style** is a reflection of your personality, your character, and how you interact with others. Your style will often impact your value to a company for a particular job. Military veterans have challenges with this, especially newly separated service members. You don't have to shed the discipline style, but you will need to decompress a bit. And yes, believe it or not, you will find it helpful to smile!

For example, if an employer needs a salesperson who will make daily cold calls, he or she will likely want a gregarious people-person who is not discouraged by refusals. If you are a soloist who likes to sit alone at a computer terminal, then that sales position may not be the right job for you! You need to take your style into account on a job-by-job basis.

Right now, grab a piece of paper or sit at a computer, and make a list under each category of what you think are your strongest points in each of these categories. You MUST take the time to determine what value you really offer the business community at large, specific industry(s), and even potential specific employers.

DO NOT GO ANY FURTHER UNTIL YOU HAVE CREATED YOUR OWN LIST OF THE THINGS THAT MAKE YOU UNIQUE AND VALUABLE!

Why You Stand Out From OTHER Job Seekers:

SKILLS:

____

____

____

EXPERIENCE/Job History:

____

____

____

EXPERTISE/Unique Special Skills:

____

____

____

STYLE/Preferred Working Modes:

____

____

____

CHAPTER TWO

YOU are the Product and YOU are the Salesperson

Once you've determined your value to the business community you're ready to step into the role of marketer and salesperson.

Remember from the Introduction that there are **Four Milestones** to an effective product sale:

1. PACKAGING—To clearly differentiate you from your competition (and the subject of this book).
2. PROMOTION—So you are broadcasting your value, NOT your resume.
3. PRODUCT DEMONSTRATION—Using innovative tools during the interview process to help you become the candidate of choice. Successfully answering critical interview questions is the secret to success in this milestone.
4. PRICING—Where your true worth to the organization is measured by your total compensation package, not just salary.

The combination of these four milestones is designed to help you achieve differentiation. Differentiation is critical to ensure you stand out as the candidate of choice from the herd of other job applicants.

Another way of describing differentiation is branding or packaging.

Yes, I know you are not a tube of toothpaste or a fast-food chain. And I know it may be tempting to skip this step and go right to writing resumes and learning job interview techniques. But it doesn't matter whether you agree or like the idea.

Differentiation, branding, and packaging have become critical in successful job searches.

Tom Peters, in his 1997 *Fast Company* magazine article titled "The Brand Called You" (http://www.fastcompany.com/magazine/10/brandyou.html) said:

> *"We are CEOs of our own companies: Me Inc. Create a message and a strategy to promote the brand called You. ... You're every bit as much a brand as Nike, Coke, Pepsi, or the Body Shop. To start thinking like your own favorite brand manager, ask yourself the same question the brand managers at Nike, Coke, Pepsi, or the Body Shop ask themselves: What is it that my product or service does that makes it different?"*

Don't get lost in the pile with everyone else's resumes and cover letters! Be seen as a solution to the company's problems and not another piece of paper!

Personal branding involves taking control of how you are perceived. So whether or not you like it or were aware of it, you already have a brand. Your brand is the combination of personal attributes, values, strengths, and passions that represent the value you offer. So it's up to you to identify those qualities and characteristics within you, bring all the pieces together, and communicate a crystal clear, consistent message that differentiates your unique promise of value and resonates with your target employer.

I do not know where you are in the process or familiarity with selling, but there are several good books on personal branding including:

- *The Complete Idiot's Guide to Branding Yourself* by Sherry Beck Paprocki
- *Me 2.0, Revised and Updated Edition: 4 Steps to Building Your Future* by Dan Schawbel
- *Branding Yourself: How to Use Social Media to Invent or Reinvent Yourself* by Erik Deckers and Kyle Lacy (Que Biz-Tech)
- *You Are a Brand!: How Smart People Brand Themselves for Business Success* by Catherine Kaputa
- *Career Distinction: Stand Out by Building Your Brand* by William Arruda and Kirsten Dixson

YOUR MARKETING TOOLBOX

Building your package or brand takes tools. After analyzing what did and did not work in the Packaging milestone for job seekers, I discovered that there are **eight key tools** every job seeker should have in his or her toolbox.

TOOL NUMBER 1: YOUR 10-SECOND COMMERCIAL

Yup, just like toothpaste and fast food, you need a commercial to communicate your brand. You will use this commercial when meeting new people, networking, and in your interviews. You want to control the perception of others and that takes a ten-second commercial that allows you to communicate your value from Chapter 2.

You want to give a positive, confident statement that explains your **expertise;** in other words, your specialized skill sets. I know it's hard to do that when you've been out of work for a while, or you have recently transitioned or are in the process of transitioning from the military, but it's important to remember that you're still the same person with the same skills and expertise you had when you were employed or were in the service.

When responding to the question "What do you do?" you don't want to respond with a statement like: "Well, I just got laid off and I'm looking for a job. Do you know anybody that's hiring?" This response is negative in its tone and almost always makes people feel uncomfortable. You also don't want to say, "Well, I was a sales manager before they laid me off." Again, a negative response. You should respond with something like, "I'm a senior sales manager looking to continue my career here in the local area. At the moment, I'm targeting some specific companies and industries to learn about potential opportunities."

There's a big difference between a positive and negative response. Let me give you a personal example. If someone were to say to me, "Nice to meet you Tom, what do you do?" I would respond, "I'm a military professional. I enjoy leading teams and people to a winning end." Or, "I am in the military and soon will be transitioning into the project management field where I can best capitalize on the skills and training I learned in the service." No bull here, just straight talk that will lead to follow-up questions.

Too many people in transition fall into the habit of responding to the "What do you do?" question by saying "I **Was** …" instead of "I **Am** …" Your expertise is current! It didn't end when you left your last employer or transitioned out of the service. Remember, you're a professional and veteran first and someone else's employee second.

Be prepared to expand your ten-second USP commercial if asked to introduce yourself to a group. This often occurs in network meetings, and in that setting, a longer introduction is expected and appropriate. No stammering allowed here. Stand proud and use the speech I used: "I am an experienced military professional who is an expert in . . . " Then simply share your expertise and skills.

Note: You may have heard the term "elevator speech" or 90-second commercial, but in my opinion you need to get sufficient information across in a much shorter period of time, especially when networking one-on-one. You want to be succinct and professional and talking too much or too long may be perceived as a negative by the other party. Just try talking for 90 seconds straight in the mirror. It feels like an eternity. Ten seconds is a snap and will allow you to maneuver into more strategic conversations.

TOOL NUMBER 2: PERSONAL BUSINESS CARDS

In Victorian England it was expected that people would carry calling cards, personal cards that included their contact information. These cards were presented when meeting someone for the first time, often delivered on a silver tray carried by the butler! This was considered good manners and provided a reference and memory tickler after the meeting/interview was concluded.

Guess what? What's old is new again! Using a personal card is so unique that it will leave an impression on everyone you contact in your job search!

Please note that we are not talking about a business card from your current or previous employer! This is a personal card that simply includes your name, designations (if any), personal contact information as well as your functional expertise. For example, your personal card should have your name, telephone, e-mail, social media (if appropriate), and your area of expertise, such as operations management, logistics management or supply chain management, etc. Including your home address is optional. The goal is to give the recipient a way to contact, you so just telephone and e-mail may be sufficient.

James R. Doe
Logistics Management

155 Anystreet
Anytown, NY 10004

Home: 555-555-1234
Mobile: 555-555-2345

Email: xxxxxxx@xxx.com
LinkedIn: www.LinkedIn.com/In/JohnRDoe

You don't need logos and fancy borders to make a good impression. Keep it simple and classic. White or ivory is best unless your industry expects wild and creative. Invest a few dollars and order cards that are on heavier stock.

Another alternative is business-card sized note cards from companies like http://www.Levenger.com. They come in both business card and 3 x 5 card sizes. You can use them like note cards for leaving messages or providing information to people you meet. WARNING: Don't use Internet providers of free business cards. While you may have a choice of designs, logos, etc., many people select the same format. These cards, in my opinion, generally look tacky and are unprofessional. Not only do they have the provider's name on the back of the business card, e.g., "free business cards at www.xyz.com," they may be flimsy and printed on cheap stock. This is not the impression you want to give. And don't print them on your home computer. Spend $50 and get 500 cards that look great. Staples, Office Max, and local print shops can assist you.

We in the military have always had a sharp image. We know how to dress and act. You wear a uniform in the military. And you will be wearing a uniform in the civilian sector as well, just a different style. Capitalize on that. Create a card that is simple, clean, and crisp. Don't let anyone talk you into color, strange designs, or cutesy logos.

Your e-mail also has to be professional. WhosYourDaddy@vvvvv.com is not at all professional for job hunting. JohnJSmith@gmail.com or JaneJDoe@gmail.com is all you need. You may want to get a new, free Google Gmail account and attach the Google Voice option to it to ensure you don't miss calls!

TOOL NUMBER 3: RESUMES

Resumes and cover letters have been around since dinosaurs roamed the corporate earth. And like most traditions, they remain necessary components of your marketing toolbox.

You will need resumes and cover letters as part of your Packaging. However, DO NOT cling to the belief that your resume alone will get you in the door. The myth of the perfect or "killer" resume is just that, a myth. The truth is it's not happening like that in today's economy.

You will read more about an effective addition to your resume that will aid in your job search success in the next section. But here we describe the necessary evil that is a resume.

Regardless of how professional your resume looks, how incredible your experience and accomplishments, how stunning your education, etc., your resume is just one of thousands and thousands and thousands. There is **no** differentiation—you just look like everyone else out there begging for a job.

Yes, I know that there is that rare individual whose resume hits the right desk at the right time and they get the dream job. I also hear about people winning the lottery or progressive slot machines for millions of dollars. But I wouldn't want to build my financial future on those rare examples and neither should you rely on just your resume winning the job lottery.

Regardless of the content, format, and presentation, your resume represents nothing more than a reflection of the past. Yet companies are interested in what you can do for them moving forward.

Resumes are backward-looking not forward-looking.

Here's my favorite definition of a resume from my co-author Greg Wood:

> *"Resume (rez-uh-may): a necessary evil. A brief written account of professional qualifications, experience, accomplishments, and education that usually invites rejection from potential employers. Old-fashioned; generally lacking in effectiveness."*

This may be one of the hardest things for veterans to understand. We in the military have never needed a paper resume to introduce ourselves. We "read" resumes dozens of times a day and did it from 100 feet away! All we had to do was look at a person's chest to see where and what they have done, and look on the collar or sleeve to see rank and position. Everyone knows who you are while in the military.

But civilian employers like paper resumes. So get your thoughts on paper as previously discussed and seek advice. There are thousands of folks like me willing to assist. Don't sweat the load too much.

Professional resume writers can be a significant help to you if you have not prepared a resume for quite some time or are not sure of your ability to present yourself in the right way. If you know you have poor writing skills or English is a second language for *you*, you may need to have a professional prepare your resume. Just be sure it can be easily read and gets your information across in an accurate and concise way. And don't forget, regardless of who prepares your resume, several pairs of eyes are needed to review your final resume before you send it out.

Be forewarned however, about resume services. I have worked with thousands of job seekers over the years and many of them have shown me resumes that have cost them anywhere from $75 to $500 or more. A fair number of these professionally prepared resumes had spelling, grammatical, and format errors. Before agreeing to work with one of these professionals, be sure to ask for references and samples of their **Military Veteran** resumes.

Your biggest obstacle in using a resume as the lone tool for finding your next job is human resources. That's where a resume ends up. HR's job is to wrangle and strangle resumes. And that is assuming your perfectly crafted, beige, parchment paper resume gets past the new "meatgrinder" software it was scanned into and ends up in the hands of a real person! Virtually all companies with more than 25 employees now use meatgrinder software to eliminate candidates whose resumes lack the right keywords and longtail phrases.

The bottom line is, your resume does a lousy job of conveying your value to a potential employer. However, a professional resume is a tradition and is simply a necessary evil; therefore yours must be a professional representation of your work experience, areas of expertise, accomplishments, and education.

There are three popular types of resumes: the chronological, combination, and functional resume. Included in the next chapter are samples of these resumes and explanations on how to create them. Use the examples as you create your own resume.

TOOL NUMBER 4: THE BIOGRAPHY

The biography is an essential component of your marketing toolbox and is an innovative tool that will clearly differentiate you from your competition. This is the sniper rifle in your arsenal of weapons. This unique tool is targeted specifically toward hiring managers in companies of interest and allows you to customize your approach by focusing on what you can do for that particular company moving forward.

Remember, your resume is nothing more than a reflection of the past and does a lousy job of conveying your potential value to an organization. This is the most effective tool I have ever used in civilian job hunting and I have found it continues to be the best tool to differentiate you from the rest of the herd of commodity job seekers.

To be effective, your biography should be a brief, one-page summary of your professional background. People often ask me what they should include in a biography. You're probably wondering the same thing.

Let me suggest this scenario: Imagine that you're having a cup of coffee with a hiring manager who works for a company that you're interested in. This isn't an interview, it's a casual meeting. In the middle of the conversation, he or she asks "Tell me, how can you help our company?" You're not going to respond to this question by reciting your resume. Instead, you're going to present yourself in a conversational way, discussing how your skills, experience, accomplishments and personal style could represent **added value** to this potential employer. What you say in this conversation becomes the foundation of your biography.

The biography is completely free-form, so you need to think about how you can best present what **you** offer to the marketplace in terms of your **value**. Typically, it should include a general summary of your experience and expertise, perhaps several soft skills, highlights or accomplishments (from any period in your career), and a generic forward-thinking statement—what you want to do next. In a biography, you don't have to mention names of the companies you worked for or even the industry you worked in.

There is no set format to the biography, so it can be all text, mostly bullets, or a combination of both. It's written in third person as if someone else is presenting you to the reader. For example, "Mr. Jones is an accomplished team builder ...," or "Ms. Smith earned her MBA..."

I prefer a shorter biography (using an opening paragraph, several bullets, and a closing paragraph), compared to a full page of text. But remember, it's your choice.

More information on the biography, along with a sample and associated cover letters, can be found in **SECTION 2** *Fire Your Resume!* in this book. You will find a sample biography in the following chapter. Be sure to look it over.

TOOL NUMBER 5: COVER LETTERS

Too many people use one standard letter. Whether using a traditional letter or strategic networking letter, make sure your cover letters are personalized to your targeted audience. Whether you're sending it to human resources, referral contacts, or a hiring manager, make sure you tailor it to that person. Be sure it gets your point across in a concise way that demonstrates self-confidence. Included in the next chapter are samples of these cover letters and explanations on how to create them. Use the examples as you create your own letter.

TRADITIONAL RESUME COVER LETTERS

These particular letters begin by referring to the position you're applying for and its job code (if indicated). The meat of each letter demonstrates how your qualifications match the key job requirements, as listed in the ad. If the ad requests a salary history, give a range rather than a specific number. Unfortunately, whether you include or omit salary information, you still run the risk of being screened out.

End your letters with a closing statement expressing your eagerness to move forward to the interview process.

STRATEGIC COVER LETTERS

Strategic cover letters are used to gather information as well as contact potential employers. These are usually requests for general information on the company or the industry. They are also used to request networking leads or contact someone to whom you were referred for additional information.

Most of the strategic cover letters here are **NOT** a request for a job interview or anything related to employment with that company! While you will include a biography or other general information, you will NOT include a resume. Resumes

scream "I need a job" and you are **NOT** job hunting with the recipient. You **ARE** information hunting.

As with your resume, biography, and any other correspondence you may send, make sure your cover letters are accurate in terms of spelling and grammar.

Note: Included with TheHireRoad™ are numerous sample cover letters. These include traditional and strategic networking letters. Like other sample documents, they are in Word format, so you can easily customize them. Samples of the following letters are included in Chapter 3 of this book:

Traditional Cover Letters

Resume Cover Letters

Strategic Cover Letters

Sample Strategic Value Letter

Sample Strategic Job Listing Letter

Strategic Networking Letter

Meeting Letter

Referral Letter

Research Letter

TOOL NUMBER 6: MANAGEMENT ENDORSEMENTS

If the biography is the sniper rifle in your arsenal then your management endorsements are your artillery or air cover. It's a killer during any interview and usually blows away the interviewer. As a consumer, think about how you choose to buy one product over another. We're all influenced by product endorsements which cause us to favor one particular product over another. In the context of job search, the same is true for hiring decisions. Awards, letters of recommendation, certificates of achievement, and accolades extracted from your past performance reviews all endorse you as a candidate. You can also attain these from fitness reports and military award citations. These may strongly influence the hiring manager to select **you** over others.

Think about how you are influenced by testimonials and product reviews on websites and advertisements. Hiring managers are looking for similar validation and decision shortcuts! If other managers like you, you are less of a risk if hired. Think of management endorsements and awards as your equivalent of the Good Housekeeping Seal of Approval on your career.

Dig out past copies of your reviews and look for any statements made by former managers that are praiseworthy. Take four or five of those statements verbatim and list them on a single sheet of paper, in quotes. Be sure to identify the name, title, and company of the person who made the statement. You don't need to list a date.

Your management endorsements can reflect any period in your career. When reviewing performance reviews, look for those areas where you received a high mark or statements of praise that former managers have made concerning your performance. Make a note of these. Also make a list of any awards that you've received, such as employee of the month, year, etc.

Remember, you're entitled to copies of signed performance reviews, so if you can't locate your own copies, contact your former managers, and/or HR departments, and request them.

Take advantage of your management endorsements. You can paraphrase them in cover letters, resumes, and biographies, and you can take advantage of the actual wording of endorsements during the interview. You'll reinforce your value and provide additional reasons for the hiring manager to select **you** as the preferred solution.

If you are still on good terms with your previous employer and/or supervisors, you can ask them for current letters or e-mails. Don't be shy about asking for their help! Most managers are happy to assist within the restrictions of any rules and regulations.

Your management endorsements represent a fantastic tool to introduce during the all-important strategic interview and will clearly separate you from your competition. Samples of this tool along with an explanation of the strategy can be found in TheHireRoad™ job search tutorial.

TOOL NUMBER 7: THE POST-INTERVIEW PACKET

The post-interview packet is another innovative tool that should definitely be included in your marketing toolbox and will clearly put you head and shoulders above other candidates competing for the same job. Numerous clients have said that it was the post-interview packet that got them their job. It further differentiates you from the pack like the biography and management endorsements did on the front end.

This tool is sent directly to the hiring manager once the entire interview process is complete. While other candidates will be sending a typical thank-you letter, thank-you card, or—God forbid—an impersonal thank-you e-mail, you'll be providing a complete packet to the hiring manager that contains everything he or she needs to know to make the decision to hire YOU. The post-interview packet is generally made up of five sections:

1. Value Proposition (written in first person)
2. Biography and Resume
3. Management Endorsements
4. Education, Certifications, and Additional Training
5. References

Completed and sent overnight following the last interview in the process, the post-interview packet is designed to be sent directly to the manager who is making the decision to hire. If it's going to be a collaborative decision between several managers, send each a packet.

Your post-interview packet should be professionally presented in an inexpensive presentation folder, preferably with a clear cover. Use dividers or heavier card stock to label and separate each section.

Your target is the hiring manager, **NOT** human resources.

Hand-written thank-you cards should be sent to all others you met during the interview process. Personalize each of these cards by referring to something unique about each person you met. I would encourage you to avoid sending an e-mail thank-you. I believe they're impersonal and typically get lost in the myriad of e-mails that busy managers receive every day.

Your post-interview packet should include a cover letter which expresses your appreciation for the opportunity to interview, your interest in the company and the position, your reference to the enclosed interview packet, and your keen interest in entertaining an offer. End the letter with a statement that implies that, after receiving an offer, you look forward to being part of the organization and making an immediate contribution.

TOOL NUMBER 8: REFERENCES

Keep in mind that references are not the same as endorsements. References are generally used to validate employment in terms of title, length of employment, salary, and eligibility for rehire. Endorsements are awards, letters of recommendation, statements of praise, etc.

While you may already have an established list of references, it may change based on the discussion during the interview. For example, the hiring manager mentions a former manager of yours that he knows. If this former manager represents a good reference for you, you want to be sure to include his or her name on your list. Also keep in mind that a prospective employer may want additional contacts above and beyond your list, including one or two personal ones. Always follow their lead in providing the right type of references.

It's a good idea to maintain an up-to-date list reference list that you can use at any time. Be sure to notify those contacts before they receive a call from your potential employer and agree on the information to be provided.

ADDITIONAL MARKETING TOOLS

SALES LITERATURE

Sales literature includes flyers or brochures which may be helpful if you're attempting to promote yourself as an independent consultant. If you're going to develop such tools, make sure they are professional in both content and appearance. This includes the correct grammar and no spelling errors.

PORTFOLIO OF SAMPLE WORK

This is a useful tool when applying for positions that involve creativity and design. For example, if you're applying for a marketing position, you want to present samples that display your writing, design, and creative talents. If you're applying for a web developer position, provide specific examples of websites. These could be either on CD or live.

Review all the tasks you did in the military and recent civilian employment. Maybe you assisted in the development of a new methodology for utilizing UAV's or you rewrote the Safety SOP for your unit. Have copies if possible so you can show your work.

CHAPTER THREE

Creating a Resume and Cover Letter

There are three typical resume formats: Chronological, Functional, and Combination:

THE CHRONOLOGICAL RESUME

The **Chronological** resume is most commonly used when your work experience reflects significant time, and perhaps advancement, with each employer. Such experience prepares you well for the type of job you're seeking. This format is also the most preferred by HR departments.

Note: Make sure you use the format preferred by each employer. Some will have specific requirements for submission. If in doubt, ask the human resources department at each employer what they want from a job applicant. Simply asking can help differentiate you from the hundreds that don't!

THE FUNCTIONAL RESUME

If you're new to the job market, you're changing careers, or you have gaps in employment, the **Functional** resume will probably be a better choice. This format is typically used to highlight accomplishments that are broken down by function. Unlike the chronological resume, it doesn't focus on soft skills, employers, responsibilities, and dates of employment. Instead, your accomplishments and expertise are listed on the first page with your work experience listed in reverse chronological order on the second page, along with your education, certifications, etc. While you may be tempted to omit specific dates of employment, this omission may lead employers to think that you're withholding something.

THE COMBINATION RESUME

The **Combination** resume is a blend of both chronological and functional formats. With this format you're able to highlight those skills that are relevant to your current search by placing them in a special section by function to draw the reader's attention.

See examples of these resumes on the following pages.

SAMPLE CHRONOLOGICAL RESUME

YOUR NAME

1212 Anystreet
Anytown, CA 55555

Cell: (555) 555-5555
Email: xxxxxxx@ gmail.com

PERSONNEL MANAGEMENT

Accomplished professional offering significant experience and expertise in Personnel Management. Skilled in the development of personnel systems and strategies that adhere to corporate objectives. Strong ability to implement a modern leadership style/structure to accomplish productivity goals through effective supervision and teamwork. Highly motivated with an aptitude for mitigating risks while effectively working with senior management, internal employees and service personnel to establish and maintain a positive work environment. Demonstrated ability to meet and exceed performance objectives. Additional strengths include:

- Analytical/Problem Solving
- Organizational Skills
- Communication Skills
- Training & Development
- Project Implementation
- Process Improvement

PROFESSIONAL EXPERIENCE

MAXWELL AIR FORCE BASE – Alabama **2003 – 2012**

Air Force's center for Joint Professional Military Education

PERSONNEL MANAGER

Responsible for overseeing personnel programs and policies for over 2,500 base employees.

- Led the implementation of a personnel management process that resulted in a 35% increase in staff efficiency.
- Coached, trained and developed processes and people within the location which led to knowledgeable and engaged employees. Achieved a 97.3% graduation rate.
- Worked with the Employment Practices Assessments (EPA), and Affirmative Action planning which ensured OFCCP compliance and OSHA compliance.
- Reformulated recruitment procedures resulting in a 30% improvement of successful new hires.
- Redesigned and implemented orientation packages resulting in faster integration of new contracted hires.

TRAVIS AIR FORCE BASE – California **2001 - 2003**

United States Air Force air base under the operational control of the Air Mobility Command (AMC)

ASSISTANT PERSONNEL MANAGER

Responsible for the coordination and follow-up of assigned tasks to ensure timely and cost-efficient completion of projects.

- Addressed and resolved salary issues relating to base contracted personnel.
- Acted in a supervisory role with management and support staffs.
- Responsible for the hiring of additional contracting staff as well as termination procedures when necessary.
- Coordinated the preparation of briefs for senior management.

SAMPLE CHRONOLOGICAL RESUME

YOUR NAME **PAGE 2**

EDUCATION & TRAINING

Bachelor of Science (BS) – Business Administration
George Mason University – Fairfax, VA

Completion of the following programs sponsored by the Air Force:

Computer Data Handling
Human Resource Management
Management Communications

Junior Executive Training Academy
US Air Force Training Command – Montgomery, AL

Junior Management Training Academy
US Air Force Training Command – Montgomery, AL

US Air Force Recruit Training
US Air Force Training Command – Orlando, FL

COMPUTER SKILLS

OPERATING SYSTEMS
Windows (9X, 2000, ME, XP, Vista), Linux, UNIX, MS DOS

MS OFFICE
Word, Excel, Access, PowerPoint, Outlook / Outlook Express

COMMENDATIONS / AWARDS

Two Letters of Commendation for superior performance and leadership
Two Achievements Awards for exceeding recruiting goals

Typical traditional, same-old resume format

SAMPLE FUNCTIONAL RESUME

YOUR NAME

1212 Anystreet
Anytown, CA 55555

Cell: (555) 555-5555
Email: xxxxxxx@ gmail.com

LOGISTICS MANAGEMENT

Accomplished professional offering solid experience and expertise in logistical functions that are readily transferable to the civilian sector. Highly skilled in the coordination and execution of tasks to ensure the timely delivery of materials and resources. Detail-oriented team leader with a strong ability to review and continually improve operational plans to adhere to established objectives while increasing efficiency and profitability. Demonstrated ability to meet and exceed performance objective, many times with limited resources. Additional strengths include:

- Analytical/Problem Solving
- Organizational Skills
- Vendor Relations
- Training & Development
- Process Improvement
- Communication Skills

EXPERTISE & KEY ACCOMPLISHMENTS

LOGISTICS MANAGEMENT

- Coordinated the redistribution of 3,400 supply items which resulted in an approximate cost savings of $45,000.
- Received Letter of Commendation in 2009 for superior performance.
- Assisted in directing logistics support operations involving 6 Federal Aviation Administration sites.
- Coordinated logistics support during wartime, including equipment and resupply.
- Developed and implemented a logistics plan to support a capacity expansion from 185,000 tons to 275,000 tons.
- Facilitated team charged with the improvement of inventory and integrity record accuracy, resulting in improved on-time delivery from 35% to 85%.

MANAGEMENT AND SUPERVISION

- Processed 200-300 arrival files per month, ensuring data in Base Operations Tracking System was accurate and up-to-date.
- Supervised staff in the creation of working plans which incorporated internal & external customer requirements.
- Monitored accurate completion of proper government billing documents and associated files to be submitted to various relevant parties, resulting in a 20% cost-savings per month. Earned special recognition from the organization's President.

TRAINING & DEVELOPMENT

- Routinely trained incoming staff on order placement and inventory control.
- Designed and implemented training program to maintain relationships with more than 65 suppliers to ensure sufficient inventory levels during intermittent budgetary restrictions.

SAMPLE FUNCTIONAL RESUME

YOUR NAME **PAGE 2**

PROFESSIONAL EXPERIENCE

HILL AIR FORCE BASE - Utah **2009 – 2012**
One of three Air Force Materiel Command logistics centers
LOGISTICS MANAGER

ROBINS AIR FORCE BASE - Georgia **2003 – 2009**
One of three Air Force Materiel Command logistics centers
LOGISTICS SUPERVISOR

EDUCATION & TRAINING

Bachelor of Science (BS) – Business Administration
George Mason University – Fairfax, VA

Completion of the following programs sponsored by the Air Force:

Computer Data Handling
Human Resource Management
Management Communications

Junior Executive Training Academy
US Air Force Training Command – Montgomery, AL

Junior Management Training Academy
US Air Force Training Command – Montgomery, AL

US Air Force Recruit Training
US Air Force Training Command– Orlando, FL

COMPUTER SKILLS

OPERATING SYSTEMS
Windows (9X, 2000, ME, XP, Vista), Linux, UNIX, MS DOS

MS OFFICE
Word, Excel, Access, PowerPoint, Outlook / Outlook Express

COMMENDATIONS / AWARDS

Two Letters of Commendation for superior performance and leadership
Two Achievements Awards for exceeding recruiting goals

SAMPLE COMBINATION RESUME

YOUR NAME

1212 Anystreet
Anytown, CA 55555

Cell: (555) 555-5555
Email: xxxxxxx@ gmail.com

INFORMATION TECHNOLOGY

Accomplished professional offering significant experience and expertise in the translation of business issues into business solutions through the effective implementation of information technology. Strong focus on increased productivity, efficiency and cost reduction. An effective leader with exceptional communication and presentation skills. Additional strengths include:

- Emerging Technologies
- Budget Management
- Training & Development
- Vendor Management

SELECTED ACCOMPLISHMENTS

COST SAVINGS ª PRODUCTIVITY ª TRAINING

- **Contributed to a savings of approximately $325,000** by implementing new software package that increased base-wide operational efficiencies.
- **Reduced costs by 27%** through the implementation of new PCs in conjunction with new host system.
- **Saved an estimated annual cost of $84,000** by overhauling antiquated EDI system.
- **Achieved a 24% increase in productivity** through the implementation of a company wide wireless two-way communication solution.
- **Enabled estimated $1.2 million savings since first quarter 2009 while enhancing productivity** by evaluating and deploying hand-held wireless two-way communication solution.
- **Recognized as a team player** who requires minimal supervision, demonstrating the highest levels of commitment and integrity.
- **Received two Letters of Commendation** for exceptional performance in the training of junior staff.

PROFESSIONAL EXPERIENCE

HHC WORLDWIDE - Santa Ana, CA **2008 – 2012**
Major provider of technology support for small to mid-size organizations throughout the U.S.
IT SPECIALIST

- Ensured effective Information Technology education, promotion, implementation, and communication throughout entire company.
- Diagnosed major system problems and implemented solutions in offices throughout the United States.
- Assisted in the recruitment, hiring and development of junior IT staff. Managed cross-departmental training in office automation and information management tools.

SAMPLE COMBINATION RESUME

YOUR NAME **PAGE 2**

MILITARY EXPERIENCE

MACDILL AIR FORCE BASE - Florida
US Air Force (2002 – 2008)

EDUCATION & TRAINING

Bachelor of Science (BS) – Business Administration
George Mason University – Fairfax, VA

Completion of the following programs sponsored by the Air Force:

Computer Data Handling
Human Resource Management
Management Communications

Junior Executive Training Academy
US Air Force Training Command – Montgomery, AL

Junior Management Training Academy
US Air Force Training Command – Montgomery, AL

US Air Force Recruit Training
US Air Force Training Command– Orlando, FL

COMPUTER SKILLS

OPERATING SYSTEMS
Windows (9X, 2000, ME, XP, Vista), Linux, UNIX, MS DOS

MS OFFICE
Word, Excel, Access, PowerPoint, Outlook / Outlook Express

COMMENDATIONS / AWARDS

Two Letters of Commendation for superior performance and leadership
Two Achievements Awards for exceeding recruiting goals

TECHNICAL SKILLS

- Software Development
- EDI (Electronic Data Interchange)
- Network & Systems Planning
- Windows XP/NT/9x
- MS Office, Visio, Project
- LAN/WAN Infrastructure
- Visual Basic, SQL
- Intranet, Extranet

There are hundreds of books and websites with suggested formats for resumes. Generally they will include sections including:

OBJECTIVE

While you may choose to have "Summary of Qualifications" or "Objective" at the top of your resume, remember you won't get more than a 15 to 30 second glance. HR is **not** going to take the time to read a summary paragraph to determine your specialized skills or expertise. I don't like objectives at the top of a resume. If it doesn't match that of the company with regard to the position you're applying for, you're rejected right away. They'll move right on to the next resume on the top of the stack. So therefore, in my opinion, replace "Summary of Qualifications" or "Objective" with your current title, the title you're seeking, or your expertise.

AREA OF EXPERTISE

The very top should include your **NAME** and all **CONTACT** information. Below your contact information I would suggest you list, in bold, capital letters your area of **EXPERTISE**. This could be your title in your current or last position, the title you are seeking or your expertise in general. For example, you could have "Supply Chain Manager" as a title or "Supply Chain Management" as an area of expertise.

As a military veteran you will need to avoid ALL abbreviations or insider terms. Terms like "Platoon Sergeant" or "EOD Team Lead" will confuse most recipients and get you passed over. But "Explosive Ordnance Team Manager" or "Helicopter Mechanic" will more clearly specify what title you have or have held.

THREE OR FOUR SENTENCE DESCRIPTION OF EXPERIENCE

Listed below your expertise or title, you will want to provide three or four sentences describing your general experience and skills. As a rule of thumb, don't ever include anything on your resume that can be used as a reason to **not** hire you. For example, beginning your summary with "Over 35 years experience …" gives away your age immediately and can certainly work against you.

SKILLS

Listed below your description of skills and experience should be your key strengths or competencies. These are transferable or soft skills, represented by four to six bullet points.

PROFESSIONAL EXPERIENCE

Listed below these soft skills is your professional experience, presented in chronological order beginning with your current or most recent employer. When you make a list of your years of experience, keep in mind that potential employers are only interested in what you've done over the last 12 to 15 years or so.

If you've had several positions with the same employer over a period of years, be sure to list the total number of years to the right of the employer name and location, and then the years in each position next to each title. Avoid listing the years for each position on the right side of the resume since it will create the impression of job-hopping, another reason to screen you out.

Note: You should only list years of employment, not months. If you list months, it can be detrimental to you in terms of creating the impression that you're a job-hopper. For example, if the length of employment was from November 2002 to January 2003, to the reader this indicates no more than three months of employment, which may lead to speculation as to the short tenure. However, this short term of employment could have been the result of circumstances beyond your control.

However, if you list 2002 to 2003, this could theoretically mean almost two full years of employment. The point is, if a hiring manager wants to know the specific time you spent with any employer, he or she will ask during the interview.

When you list each employer, indicate the type of business. Below that, list your most recent title and provide a one or two sentence description of your general responsibilities.

ACCOMPLISHMENTS

In the context of your resume, accomplishments are things you've done that have benefited your employer. An easy way to state your accomplishments is to use the acronym P.A.R., which stands for problem, action, and results. For example:

Resolved customer service issues by creating new policies and procedures that resulted in a 40% decrease in customer complaints.

The "P," or problem, was the customer service issue; the "A," or action, was creating new policies and procedures, and the "R," or result, was a 40 percent decrease in customer complaints. Keeping your accomplishments up to P.A.R. is an easy way for you to explain how you have benefited your employer. When you list your accomplishments always try to begin each with an action verb.

When using P.A.R., you can list your problem, action, and results in any order, as long as you include all three elements. Let me give you an example:

Achieved a 40% reduction in customer complaints by implementing new policies and procedures which effectively addressed existing customer service issues,

or

Achieved a 100% job completion rate by training teams to maximize their peak efficiencies while working in a high risk and physically dangerous environment.

(Meaning you kicked ass while in a combat high risk environment...Good on ya!)

This sequence is R.A.P. (Result, Action, and Problem).

For each employer, try to quantify your accomplishments using any type of numbers, such as percentages, dollars, quantities (doubled, tripled, etc.). Include one or two accomplishments for each year you worked for the company, listing them under the corresponding titles or positions you held. Civilians love numbers so try to make sure you have dollars signs ($), percentages (%) and other measurements in your resume if at all possible.

EDUCATION

If you've earned a college degree, indicate the name of the college, city and state, and degree earned. If you've earned several degrees, list the most advanced degree first. If you've attended some college, but did not earn a degree, be sure to list the college name, city, and state, and the focus of the coursework. If you're a high school graduate and have not attended any college, list your high school and city and state. If you've attended college, even for any period of time, you need not include your high school education. If you have additional training, technical skills, and/or certifications, list these below the description of your education.

If you have recently been in the military, you may choose to list this experience under a separate heading of Military History or leave it under the educational heading. Translate those military schools you have attended into a civilian equivalent such as: Staff NCO (non-commissioned officer) Academy, which is the equivalent of Junior Management Training.

PERSONAL INFORMATION

Do **NOT** list any personal information, such as marital status, number of children, hobbies or interests unless the information is pertinent to the specific opportunity. References should **NOT** be listed on your resume. They should be presented at the appropriate time, which we'll discuss later.

MORE YOU SHOULD KNOW ABOUT RESUMES

There are a variety of things on your resume that could screen you out. It could be your name, which may indicate a certain ethnic origin and, therefore, potential difficulty with the English language. It could be your address, which may trigger relocation issues. It could be your former employers and how long you worked for them, or how short a time you worked for them. It could be something that gives away your age. Other things that could screen you out could include your title, your experience, the industry you're in, your education, your lack of education, or even your affiliations.

CHECK FOR ERRORS

Make absolutely sure you check your resume for spelling and grammatical errors. Have several other people review it before submitting it to anyone. Don't rely on spell check when proofreading your resume. Remember, there are many words that can be used incorrectly that spell check will not pick up. For example, "principle software engineer" should read "principal software engineer." But since both "principle" and "principal" are both valid words with different meanings, spell check will not catch that error. Just like hanger and hangar—one is something you put clothes on the other is a place for aircraft.

There is absolutely no excuse for spelling and grammatical errors! Regardless of how professional, how impressive, and how accurate your resume is in terms of work history, it won't get you the job if it contains errors! While your resume may provide a number of potential reasons to screen you out, don't let sloppiness be the immediate cause for rejection.

TELL THE TRUTH

A few words of advice: don't ever lie or stretch the truth on your resume. Research indicates that up to 50 percent of job seekers do just that, most commonly exaggerating their education. Creative writing is something that you often find in magazines, and almost always in resumes. There are probably thousands of candidates out there who have been screened out because of their resume, but who could have won the Pulitzer Prize for fiction!

If you have been awarded a medal be proud to list it under awards and achievements. But because of stolen valor, make sure you have supporting documents like your DD-214 at the ready if challenged.

SIMPLE IS BETTER!

Don't get creative in the appearance of your resume. I suggest that you don't use brightly colored paper, shading, boxes, pretty squiggly lines or any kind of graphics. And don't include your picture which is an unnecessary distraction. These are additional reasons to screen you out!

ADDITIONAL RESUME TIPS

Stay away from resume distribution services. What these outfits do is take your money in return for bundling your resume with many others and sending them unsolicited to so-called inside contacts in companies all over the country. What do you think happens to the bundle of resumes received? You're right! They join the pile in the circular file. If you're approached by one of these resume distribution services, ask them for a sample list of their inside contacts. But don't hold your breath waiting for it!

With TheHireRoad™ job search tutorial you have the ability to create a high-impact, professional resume. Included are a number of samples of each format along with a variety of suggested templates. They are all in Microsoft Word format, so they're easy to customize. The **Resource** section of TheHireRoad™ will allow you to view and customize resumes that best fit your needs.

For more information on resumes, and why they are a LOUSY tool for job hunting, see **SECTION 2** *Fire Your Resume!* in this book.

SAMPLE BIOGRAPHY

Following is the biography for a job seeker looking for a job in information technology. It is written in the third person and focuses on his accomplishments relative to both past employment history as well as value to a similar/target employer.

Notice that it is much shorter than a traditional resume and is, in reality, a sales piece for the job seeker!

SAMPLE BIOGRAPHY - MILITARY
(INFORMATION TECHNOLOGY)

YOUR NAME

Biography

Xxxxxxx Xxxxxx is a top rated military veteran offering significant experience and expertise in Information Systems and Technology, specifically in the area of network installation, maintenance and troubleshooting. Having earned a BS degree in Computer Science, and with numerous certifications, he has spent more than eight years applying his knowledge to every facet of his trade, including the supervision and training of junior staff. In addition, Mr. Xxxxxx has experience with budgeting, project management, and employee relations, due diligence, implementations/ integrations and even site closures.

Highlights of Mr. Xxxxxx's career include:

- Received two Letters of Commendation for superior performance (2009 and 2010).
- Improved IT help desk response time taken from almost non existent to an average of 1 day for general tasks and 1 week for application development.
- Seamless transition thru proactive modification and replacement of particular legacy programs and hardware, resulting in a savings of $43,000.
- Managed multiple sites with minimal labor costs by incorporating the principles of team collaboration and hands-on management.
- Migrated and/ or integrated multiple legacy systems to newer platforms including financial systems, manufacturing systems, tracking systems and analytical processing systems. These efforts resulted in a savings of $15,000 per month while greatly improving efficiency.
- Regarded as the internal expert on data collection and complex reporting.
- Managed various levels of staff providing support and development services.

Known by most as creative, frugal, detail oriented and diligent, Mr. Xxxxxx is an articulate professional with a strong desire to excel. He works exceptionally well with diverse groups and is able to provide on-time results and reduce costs. He understands the needs of the business as well as the individuals and is never out of touch with either.

Having served in the U.S. Marine Corps, Mr. Xxxxxx brings commitment, dedication and a strong passion for excellence to his work. He is now is seeking a position with a progressive company or organization in the private sector where he can utilize his expertise in Information Systems/Technology management and, as an integral team member, achieve defined business objectives that contribute to increased profitability.

Telephone: (555) 555-5555 Email: xxxxxxx@ xxxxx.net

SAMPLE STRATEGIC VALUE LETTER

(for use with biography)

When you send a copy of your biography to a potential employer, you only have about ten seconds to make an impression on the recipient! So to help let the recipient know why you are contacting them and sending your biography, you need a short and clear cover letter.

Following is a format that has proven successful over the last twelve years with job seekers I have coached:

Date

Name
Title
Company Name
Address
City, State, Zip

Dear Mr. / Ms. Jones:

As an accomplished military veteran with many years of experience in Information Technology Management I am currently exploring opportunities within your industry, and your company is of interest to me. Please understand that I am *not* contacting you to ask for a job. My objective is to simply expand my professional network by familiarizing you with how my skills, experience and expertise could represent added value to you, and your organization, at some point in the future.

As a means of introduction I have taken the liberty of enclosing a brief one-page summary of my background that, as you can see, reflects significant experience in xxxxx, xxxxx xxxxxxxx and xxxxxxxxxxxx.

I understand your time is valuable, however I would welcome the opportunity to introduce myself to you personally, perhaps sharing a cup of coffee or allowing me to buy you lunch. Please expect a call from me within the next several days to hopefully arrange a short meeting.

(OR)

Please expect a call from me within the next few days to hopefully chat for a few minutes and answer any questions you may have about my background.

Thank you in advance for your time and consideration.

Sincerely,

Your name

Enclosure

SAMPLE STRATEGIC JOB LISTING LETTER

(for use with biography)

Follow a dual approach when responding to a job listing (regardless of where you saw it). After sending a copy of your resume and standard cover letter to human resources (along with everyone else), differentiate yourself and significantly improve your odds by sending your biography (not your resume at this point) and this Strategic Job Listing Letter directly to the hiring manager/decision maker for that position. Your goal is to get to the person who actually knows what the job will entail and what skills and expertise are needed to help solve their problems! NOTE: Your biography is never sent to human resources.

Date

Name
Title
Company Name
Address
City, State, Zip

Dear Mr. / Ms. Jones:

I understand your organization is currently seeking a Marketing Communications Manager. As an accomplished military veteran with a strong background in both strategic marketing development and communications, within your industry, I am keenly interested in pursuing this opportunity with Xxxxxxx Xxxx, Inc.

As a means of introduction I have taken the liberty of enclosing a brief one-page summary of my background which, as you can see, reflects significant experience in all areas of marketing communications management -- including expertise in the support of product revenue growth through improved reach, branding and market share; expertise which has helped increase brand awareness and enhance the bottom line.

Please note that I have in fact forwarded my resume directly to your Human Resources department as requested in your job listing. However, I would be most interested in meeting with you directly to further discuss the value I can bring to your organization with respect to this position. Please expect a call from me within the next few days to hopefully arrange a convenient time for us to get together.

Thank you in advance for your time and consideration.

Sincerely,

Your name

Enclosure

STRATEGIC NETWORKING LETTER

(for use with biography)

Date

Name
Title
Company Name
Address
City, State, Zip

Dear Mr. / Ms. Jones:

Would you be interested in expanding your professional network? With an extensive background in the xxxxxxxx industry that's exactly what I'm attempting to do by writing to you with the clear understanding that I'm *not* asking you for a job.

Recognizing how quickly the rapid changes in business and technology can affect job stability for all of us, I'm sure you'll agree that the most effective way to minimize such uncertainty is to nurture a network of professionals who share similar experience and expertise.

As a means of introduction I have taken the liberty of enclosing a brief one-page summary of my background that, as you can see, reflects significant skills, experience and expertise in your industry.

I would welcome the opportunity to get together with you to discuss how we can be of mutual benefit in maintaining the value we both represent to the business community. Please expect a call from me within the next few days to arrange a short meeting at your convenience.

Sincerely,

Your name

Enclosure

STRATEGIC MEETING LETTER

(for use with biography)

Date

Name
Title
Company Name
Address
City, State, Zip

Dear Mr. / Ms. Jones:

I am contacting you to ask for your help. With an extensive background in Xxxxxxxxx and Xxxxxxxxxx I am currently exploring opportunities within your industry and I'm gathering information from a variety of sources. I'm particularly interested in your views and perspectives with regard to some of the key challenges for companies in the industry, and your advice as to where my skills and experience may best be utilized.

As a means of introduction I have taken the liberty of enclosing a brief, one-page summary of my background that, as you can see, reflects significant expertise in all areas of xxxxxxxxxxxxx, xxxxxxxx, xxxxxxx xxxxxxxxx, and xxxxxxx.

Recognizing the value of your time I would welcome the opportunity to spend a few minutes with you, perhaps sharing a cup of coffee or allowing me to buy you lunch. I'd also like to learn about your background since, while I'm actively networking within the industry, there may be an opportunity to assist you in some way. Please expect a call from me within the next few days to hopefully arrange a short meeting at your convenience.

Thank you in advance for your time and consideration.

Sincerely,

Your name

Enclosure

STRATEGIC REFERRAL LETTER

(for use with biography)

Date

Name
Title
Company Name
Address
City, State, Zip

Dear Mr. / Ms. Jones:

I am contacting you to ask for your help. With a strong background in Product Management I am currently exploring opportunities within your industry, and I'm hoping that you may be able to suggest one or two individuals I could talk with to get further information.

As a means of introduction I have taken the liberty of enclosing a brief one-page summary of my background which, as you can see, reflects significant experience and expertise in all areas of Product Management; expertise which has helped increase brand awareness and enhance the bottom line.

I will call you within the next few days to hopefully chat for a few minutes and get the name of one or two people I could contact.

Thank you in advance for your time and consideration.

Sincerely,

Your name

Enclosure

STRATEGIC RESEARCH LETTER

(for use with biography)

Date

Name
Title
Company Name
Address
City, State, Zip

Dear Mr. / Ms. Jones:

With an extensive background in xxxxxxxx xxxxxxxxxxxx I am currently exploring new opportunities in your industry. As a result of this research I have concluded that your company, its products and its culture represent a good match for my qualifications and interests. My research has also indicated that your company may currently be facing one or more of the following challenges:

- Xxxxxxx xxxxxxxx xxx xxxxxxxxxx xxxxx, xxxxxxxxxxxx, xxx xxxxxxxx.
- Xxxxx xxxxxx xxx xxxxxxxx xx xxxxxxxxx
- Xxxxxxx xx xxxxxxxxx xxx xxxxxx xxxxx, xxxxxxxx xxx xxxxxx

As a means of introduction, I have taken the liberty of enclosing a brief summary of my background which reflects significant experience and expertise in all areas of xxxxxxxx xxxxxxxxxxxx. Such expertise would be a great asset in helping to address the challenges that I have listed, in addition to others you may be facing with respect to their impact on your bottom line.

I would welcome the opportunity to discuss in greater detail how I can bring value to your organization. Please expect a call from me within the next few days to hopefully arrange a short meeting.

Thank you in advance for your time and consideration.

Sincerely,

Your name

Enclosure

SUMMARY

Differentiation is going to be the key to your successful job search. And the first step in setting yourself apart from others is to develop the tools that you'll need to market yourself effectively. The strategic tools I've talked about in **Packaging** are dynamic and designed to help you achieve your key objective of standing out to be outstanding. They are your strategic weapons to overcome and breach the obstacles in your path.

Now that your marketing toolbox or arsenal is completed, with both traditional and innovative tools, you're ready to move on to the second milestone down TheHireRoad™ which is **Promotion**. Here's where you have a distinct choice:

Option 1: Do I fall victim to the traditional approach to finding employment by relying on my resume to get me in the door, or

Option 2: Do I decide to educate the business community by broadcasting my value, NOT my resume?

If you're tired of the C.R.A.P. approach to job search you'll choose Option 2.

You MUST learn how to broadcast your value and achieve differentiation. That is the focus of *Fire Your Resume!*, which provides compelling reasons to avoid the resume shotgun and C.R.A.P. approach. You'll learn the seven specific tactics for a successful job search and receive a sample biography and associated cover letters.

ADDITIONAL RESOURCES

There is a wide array of additional resources available with TheHireRoad™ job search system. While these are not exhaustive and are just samples, they do include templates and multiple industry examples. Keep in mind, each industry and individual needs to have a customized version of each tool.

A WORD OF CAUTION—In addition to checking spelling, grammar, and word usage, be sure that the content of your document is consistent. Make sure the dates, titles, and activities match. Remember, you will be bundling them together into a post-interview packet.

SECTION 2

Fire Your Resume!

INTRODUCTION

The world of work has changed dramatically over the past couple of decades. This is even more true for military veterans.

When you're working for someone else, it no longer matters how hard you work, how committed you are, how many hours you work, or how much money you make or save for the company. The days of working forty years and retiring with a gold watch are gone.

Unless you own the company, are an immediate family member to the owners, or you've been given a written lifetime employment agreement (which nobody ever gets), **your job is always in jeopardy**.

In light of this truth, you, as a trained military professional, actually have an advantage over other job seekers. You understand real jeopardy and you have been trained how to react and survive. So consider **SECTION 2** *Fire Your Resume!* your survival handbook for the world of civilian job hunting and successful employment!

WHO ARE YOU?

Duty, honor, service, commitment, and sacrifice. These are more than words to you; they represent the codes of conduct you embraced in order to serve this country. In this section you will learn how to transfer these highly prized attributes into civilian speak as you correspond with potential employers. These ideals can be transferred to the workplace, but you need special strategies and tactics to do so successfully.

Note: The advice in this book is applicable to all veterans looking for a job. However, if you are rated as a disabled veteran, there are additional services available for you through the Veterans Administration (VA) for training and placement. Talk to your local VA or a local advocacy group like the Disabled American Veteran or the Veterans of Foreign Wars for more information.

EVERYONE LOVES A VET BUT . . .

"Everyone loves a vet, but not everyone wants to hire one."

That's what we hear repeatedly from frustrated veterans looking for a job. And guess what? They're right!

Being a veteran isn't a plus for most employers because they don't know what being a vet brings to a job! So your mission is to use what you have learned in the military to separate yourself from the rest of the job applicants.

TRANSFORMING MILITARY SERVICE INTO CIVILIAN SPEAK

So how do you translate, and more importantly, communicate your unique value to someone who might not understand the military?

That's what we're here to do. We understand that translating your military service and skills into civilian terms can be a difficult and frustrating experience. Words have different meanings; work environments are different; chain of command is different; and friendships, teamwork, and coaching are not even close to what you experienced in the military. For example, remember in boot or officer training where you were taught team was first and to take care of each other? Quoting a veteran working for a large corporation who got downsized, "No way in hell is corporate America like that, just no way. It's all 'What's in it for me?'"

This does not mean you have to change or lower your standards of conduct. You just have to understand that your mission in the civilian world is different. Civilian employers are interested in you for one reason and one reason only: to help them solve problems and resolve issues that will lead to increased profitability. That as a goal is neither right nor wrong, it's just that your mission is now redefined.

IT'S NOT ABOUT CAREER PLANNING

Your job search mission is no longer about career planning, it's all about career coping. You must be ready to change jobs and careers on a moment's notice, because when you're working for someone else, even when you're making them money, *you're not in control*.

As global competition increases, companies continue to do more with less. Companies have a legal obligation (aka "fiduciary responsibility") to the stockholders (even if it is a single owner) to increase profits through any legal means they can. Sometimes that means downsizing, outsourcing, and reorganizing. And let's be honest—that happens in the military, too. Bases get closed, projects get cancelled, and mission skills change.

As a result of all the changes in the recent economy, there's a huge pool of talent on the street. And if you have already been looking for a job, you know it's tough and frustrating!

But here's something we want you to know: **Being a veteran means you have an advantage over other job seekers because you know how to stick it out. You understand the sense of mission. And you know how to take the information we are about to give you to succeed!**

To succeed in your job search in our new economy requires creativity and a willingness to think outside the box and apply innovative approaches. Your mission is to effectively meet the challenges of finding employment. Things have changed. Times have changed. And times are tough. So here are your new tools and a new approach to this new job reality.

Point of aim is point of impact, so let's get on with the attack.

CHAPTER FOUR

The "Traditional" Job Search Approach

Competing in today's job market is incredibly stressful. And it doesn't help when the tried and true methods just aren't working. But everyone keeps using them!

Despite being shown this fact every day, recruiters (and virtually all books on the subject) still tell you that all you need to get in the door is a great resume. Yet more and more job seekers are finding that the traditional system which relies on mass distribution of great resumes and knock 'em-dead cover letters no longer works. And for veterans who do not have the "usual" stuff to put on a resume, it's even less likely to work.

It's hard work sending out all those resumes. As a retired Marine and coauthor I know first-hand how incredibly difficult it is to find a job just using a resume.

Here's my story:

"So how the hell do I put one of these blasted things together?"

That's what I thought as I approached my first resume as a soon-to-be-retired Marine lieutenant colonel. The whole process was driving me crazy. After twenty years in the Corps I had to write a resume. What am I supposed to put where? How do I explain what I really did? Gag!

So I bought the books, researched the Internet, asked for help, and still really didn't have a good grasp on what a resume was supposed to communicate. Every resume I created was either just okay or needed rewriting. Everyone had an opinion and some even questioned what was on it.

"This can't be true!" someone said. "Not everyone gets an award from the President of the United States!" My response was, "I did." But apparently it wasn't something that impressed an employer.

I started sending out 20 to 30 resumes a week and getting little or no response. As a result, I decided to kick it up a notch and send out 40 to 50 a week! I have since learned Albert Einstein's definition of insanity: "Doing the same thing over and over again and expecting different results." Yup, I was going insane and what I was doing didn't make sense.

Maybe you've experienced the same frustration. In your frustration, or even desperation, you've considered a resume distribution service to solve your problem. Maybe you're attracted to such a service because of its "targeted approach" or "direct access to hiring managers." Some of these services tell you that your resume will "reach thousands of recruiters in your industry" or that their program "allows recruiters and HR managers to contact you instantly."

DON'T WASTE YOUR MONEY!

Do you really think your resume is going to get noticed among the thousands of others resumes these services bundle together and practically spam to HR professionals nationwide? Yeah, we didn't think you did.

Who really posts on job boards?

The **#1 dirty little secret of job hunting** is that the majority of these resume bundlers—job boards and want ads in places like Craigslist and the local newspaper—are really in the business of resume preparation, interview training, and other "services" for job seekers. They are **not** really in the business of finding you a job! After all, the job board is free so where are they making their money?

When they blast your resume out to "thousands of companies looking for your qualifications," you will get very little (if any) serious responses. That predictable lack of response gives the bundler or board owners a reason to tell you that your resume is the problem! Then they try to upsell their "professional" resume-writing services, job-search training, or their "special limited-time only gold package" and who knows what else to make a buck off your desperation and frustration.

And what is even worse, how can someone without military experience understand how the skills and talents honed in the military are transferable to the civilian employer? Odds are that unless they specialize in veteran employment, they won't have a clue.

Oh, and don't be surprised if the responses you do get all come from companies looking to train you to sell life insurance, do network marketing, work at home, attend an online school, go to a trade school, or sign-up for webinars for all manner of "opportunities."

The time you spend posting to job boards is basically wasted. The boards are more interested in selling you stuff than finding you a job!

Also, all the different job boards often simply scrape the same information from all the same sites. We have seen the same job listed on four or five different job boards as "exclusive." They often link to key employers in an area and many simply pull up the want ads from newspapers in the geographic area you specify! We have clicked on a job for a client and had it link to three different sites (planting Internet cookies each time it linked) before coming to rest on an employer site.

But what about career lists on the company websites? Aren't they legitimate?

Career pages on a company website are generally more legitimate than job boards. But they are usually the same listing you will see on the job boards. Also, the bigger the company, the more likely they are to use a computer program to assess your uploaded resume which could eliminate it before a human being ever sees it!

To put it bluntly, your resume is doing a lousy job, so:

FIRE IT!

But don't throw it in the trash! You must have a resume when asked for it. It needs to be a professional representation of your work experience, accomplishments, and education. However, while yours may even reflect attractive work experience and past performance in the military, it does little to convey the true value you bring to a particular company moving forward. It is **not** the way to successfully start the hiring process.

So when we talk about "firing" your resume, we don't want you to think you don't need a resume at all. Resumes are still a necessary evil. You'll have to present your resume at some point in the job search process, so make sure it is free of typos, grammatical errors, slang, etc. Still, your resume alone will not get the job done. We're offering a different approach, one that doesn't rely on just your resume to get you in the door. If you want to actually get hired you can't rely solely on sending in your resume in response to a job listing.

CHAPTER FIVE

Four Reasons Not to Send a Resume

The "HR black hole" is a common term used in the recruiting world that refers to the futility of sending your resume through normal channels like human resources (HR) or other internal hiring departments.

Clever job seekers think they can get noticed by sending their resume directly to hiring managers (potential bosses who ultimately make the decision to hire). However, 99 percent of the time those resumes will **also** end up back in a pipeline to the HR black hole. Sending out resumes as an initial way to get in the door is like wasting ordnance—shooting at your target with your eyes closed. Here are four reasons to save your ammo:

REASON 1—RESUMES END UP IN HUMAN RESOURCES

When you send a resume in response to a job listing, odds are your resume will end up in a stack a foot high, or in a database of thousands and will be viewed for no more than 15 to 30 seconds. In addition, your resume will be seen by someone in HR personnel—not by the hiring manager. HR does not make the hiring decision unless you're applying for a position in the personnel department.

Do you really want personnel deciding if you're valuable enough to put in front of the hiring manager for an interview, or do you want the hiring manager making that decision? Most job seekers we know want the hiring manager making that decision!

CONSIDER ALL YOUR OPTIONS
FOR USING YOUR SKILLS
IN NEW WAYS AND IN NEW ARENAS.

Even so, because you're a job seeker who's attempting to change careers, your resume will now actually be working against you. It will scream to HR staffers, "I'm changing careers" and that is **not** a good thing when you are looking for a job.

REASON 2—RESUMES ARE USED TO SCREEN YOU OUT

HR departments are inundated with resumes, so they are using today's scanning technology more and more as a filtering tool. This is especially true if you upload your resume online, but if you send in a paper resume, they will literally scan it into their system so they can run it through a software program that looks for keywords matching the job description.

While you may have solid qualifications, your resume can present many reasons to reject you, including lack of keywords and/or phrases, job history, gaps in employment, affiliations, education, and current location among others. Conversely, you may have negative keywords and dates that may be used to eliminate you. The whole HR process starts with rejection.

One of the problems with being in the 1 percent with military experience is that your keywords and the civilian keywords may not align. You need to remember to change the language to match that of the civilian population! Then you need to come to terms with this simple fact: Companies don't want to hire you! Not because you are a veteran. They just don't want to hire anyone new unless they absolutely must.

When companies have decided they must hire someone, they start by looking for a mythical person fitting a perfect description. While the job description they write is basically a wish-list, your resume must match up to as many keywords and phrases as possible in order to be moved to the short stack of applicants. And if you are using military terms it has a greater likelihood of being rejected as well.

You have been told over and over again that the best approach to get noticed and avoid rejection is to write directly to the hiring manager of a company, enclosing your powerful resume along with the best cover letter you've ever written. The harsh reality is that as soon as your resume is pulled from the envelope it makes several statements loud and clear:

"I'm leaving the military and looking for a new career…"

"I wasn't happy in the military…"

"I'm out of work (or will be) …"

"I'm looking for any job…,"

"I'm not happy with this position/employer/industry..."

"I need more money …"

"Are you doing any hiring…?"

With those ugly phrases ringing in the hiring manager's head, what does he do with your resume? It's either tossed into the trash or, most likely, forwarded to human resources where it stands an excellent chance—more than 95%—of being summarily rejected.

If you're lucky, you may get a courtesy "no thanks" letter or e-mail. But most of the time...you sit, waiting for the phone call that never comes.

REASON 3—RESUMES ARE NOT VALUE PROPOSITIONS

Resumes, though still used today, have a format that doesn't allow you to showcase your true talents. The resume's restrictive structure is merely a validation of what you've done in the past; it does **not** represent what you can do for a specific targeted company in their future.

Your value is much more than your education, military training, and track record of employment and career accomplishments which were beneficial to the military and any former employer(s). Hiring managers are not mind readers; therefore they cannot interpret information about you that doesn't appear on your resume.

When an employer decides to invest time and money to acquire your talent they're not interested in what you've done in the past, but what you can do for them now. It's all about the value you bring to the table; your ability to address the problems and challenges the company is facing that will increase profitability.

One of the rules of thumb for a successful written communication with a potential employer is to check it for symbols like dollar signs ($), percentages (%), and other direct measurements. If you don't see a liberal sprinkling of $, %, and # in your resume and other communications, go back and rethink what you did. Yes, even your jobs in the military should allow you to show how your skills and training accomplished real numbers!

Hiring managers also know that resumes are an exercise in creative writing. Many job seekers stretch the truth or outright lie on their resume in an effort to get noticed. While you may not be lying or stretching the truth, your resume is a poor representation of who you really are because its format only allows you to present your military and other civilian employment history and education, nothing more. You need to convey your value, and tell them what is in it for **them** and their company to hire you as a veteran!

Even powerful resumes, whether chronological, functional, or some combination, have the same structure for writing and presentation of content. Even when embellished with accomplishments, decorations, and jargon, it probably doesn't include the elements of "fit"—which is the most important factor in a hiring manager's decision to hire.

REASON 4—RESUMES DO NOT DIFFERENTIATE YOU

Your biggest challenge in job searching is differentiation. In other words, how do you separate yourself from everyone else in a fiercely competitive job market? Are you sure your resume makes you stand out from the crowd? Do you think listing your awards and decorations will help?

Think again. All resumes look the same, including yours.

We are absolutely sure you are using one of the classic formats for resumes that everyone is taught to follow. You're required to list your name, contact information, education, experience, references, and awards. The format hasn't changed since the 1950s.

Same old, same old.

Do you really think you'll get noticed waving your resume in the air, begging for a job among the hundreds of thousands, if not millions, of other job seekers using the same pricey linen paper in an elegant color?

Maybe you've tweaked your resume day after day, week after week, and now you probably think your resume is one in a million. Well guess what? It is—just one of millions! It's another piece of paper, another entry into the database. It is nothing unique.

No matter how professional it looks, no matter how impressive your experience, how amazing your accomplishments, how dangerous your postings, how many your decorations, or how stunning your education, your resume is a resume...is a resume…is a resume.

Regardless of its format, your resume looks like everyone else's resume. Therefore **you** look like everyone else, too. You do not stand out, even as a veteran!

Using a resume is not the way to stand out from other resume providers.

CHAPTER SIX

It's Time to Change Your Mindset!

The traditional approach to job searching, which involves spending countless hours sending hundreds of resumes in response to job postings found through Internet job boards, company websites, newspapers, trade publications, the unemployment office, or wherever they can be found, is **reactive**.

That means you are hunting and waiting for something to pop up in your line of sight. You are waiting for your "go" button to be pushed.

Being reactive can be ineffective. You are waiting on the right target to come into sight. You are waiting for someone to hit the enter key and post a job so you can leap into action and send a resume.

And if you're following the traditional approach, you are then waiting to get noticed. You're waiting for someone to find your submission and pick your resume out of the stack. You are waiting to be seen as better than the rest. You're waiting for something to happen.

You're at the "P" stage of C.R.A.P.—click, review/react, apply, pray.

You feel helpless because you are.

You are not in control.

You are waiting for the other side to make a move. And waiting for the other guy to make a move is a bad tactic for job hunting just like it was as warriors! How bad?

We know from experience that for all your hard work, the response has predictably been dismal. How many responses have you gotten for your efforts? One out of 20 resumes? One out of 50? More likely, 1 out of 100, a 1 percent response rate. And that's just to get an interview, **not** a job offer!

And nowadays if you are lucky, an auto-responder e-mail will acknowledge your submission. Then if you are very lucky, you might get a "no thanks, we are pursuing other avenues" e-mail. Forget a call or letter.

Why?

Because the odds are stacked against you, big time.

STOP WORRYING ABOUT FINDING A "JOB," AND START THINKING ABOUT YOUR EMPLOYABILITY!

You need to become **proactive**. You need to stop waiting on the call and make the call. You need to be the one being pursued, not the other way around. You need to be the aggressor. And this is where a military veteran has the advantage over the civilian!

You understand campaigns. You understand taking the initiative. You know how to suck it up and keep going. You know what it takes to win.

POINT OF AIM IS POINT OF IMPACT, SO PICK YOUR TARGET AND GO FOR IT!

Do the recon and learn the terrain. Once you understand where the jobs are hiding, your advantages will become clear!

What you need now is to change your mindset, set a strategy, and use better tactics.

And better tactics start with better information.

Believe it or not, advertised jobs only represent less than 25 percent of all open positions out there. Publicly posted jobs represent just the tip of the iceberg. **The other 75 percent or so are below the surface in what's called the hidden job market.**

We don't know about these jobs because they're not advertised. Yet these jobs are opened and filled every day. The reason for this is determined by the way companies hire. If a company has a critical position they need to fill, they have four resources to find the best candidate. In order of preference they are:

RESOURCE 1—INTERNAL CANDIDATES

This is an employer's best choice. This is literally posting the openings on a bulletin board or through company mail. However, filling internally is not always practical. Promoting someone from within usually creates another void that needs to be filled. This is especially true in smaller companies.

Tactical Idea 1: Look for smaller companies that announce promotions in the local press. When someone is promoted there is often a position they previously held available.

Tactical Idea 2: Look for announcements of new contracts, new construction, and/or new projects at companies in the local news. These are potential opportunities for jobs!

RESOURCE 2—REFERRAL/ RECOMMENDATIONS/ WORD-OF-MOUTH

This is the second-best choice. Sometimes employers will even offer bonuses to employees who recommend someone who is subsequently hired as a result of that referral. If no internal recommendations are made, the employer has two remaining options—both undesirable, but evil necessities in business—post the job and hire a recruiter.

RESOURCE 3—POSTING A JOB OPENING

This is not what a company wants to do. Posting a job triggers an avalanche of paper and e-mails into HR. Not only does this create resume overload, it can often cause the strongest candidates to be overlooked. This is not the optimum way to find the best employees.

RESOURCE 4—HIRE A RECRUITER

If a mountain of resumes has failed to yield the right candidate for the position, this leads to yet another undesirable choice for the employer. Hefty fees need to be paid to headhunters to find the right candidate. However, the more exclusive the job the more likely a recruiter is to be involved. The higher the pay, the more likely a company is to want a third-party to find and filter candidates.

Most companies fill 75 percent of their jobs through referral, recommendation, and word-of-mouth (Resource 2). Therefore, the majority of the time it's not necessary to publicly post a job opening where the general job hunting public can see it. But did you know that companies will still post jobs they already have candidates for?

The **#2 dirty little secret of job hunting** is that even though a position has been filled, companies will still post the job opening in order to comply with various hiring regulations and government policies. They may need to show community or minority outreach. If a hired candidate is a foreign national, they may need to prove to immigration that there are no American candidates equally qualified so they need tons of unqualified resumes as proof. And to ensure the widest possible visibility for the job proof, companies will use the big job boards as well as their own career pages.

Yet 99 percent of job seekers choose to focus on the 25 percent tip of the iceberg—the openly advertised jobs.

Why? Because it's easy!

How hard is it to wake up on a Monday morning, make a cup of coffee, stagger over to the computer in your bathrobe, and start to scroll down job after job after job on Internet job boards and company websites? Not very hard and therefore, not very productive!

Relying on Internet job boards is a very frustrating and unproductive exercise. You need to realize the fierce amount of competition you face for each and every one of these posted jobs you apply for. Regardless of your qualifications, your odds of getting noticed are very slim to none.

So how do you improve your odds?

You start with better strategy, superior tactics, and a change of focus.

Better strategy: While your competition will be following the traditional C.R.A.P. approach to finding a job, you're going to implement a strategic approach that will focus on differentiation. The success of your mission will result from your ability to clearly separate yourself from all others in today's highly competitive job market.

Superior tactics: Instead of spending all your time playing the Internet Lottery (wasting ordnance), you'll be educating the business community about who you are and the value you bring to the table as a veteran. As you develop your professional network and start to connect with hiring managers, you'll be employing innovative tools that we call your "weapons of choice," including your biography, strategic cover letters, management endorsements, and post-interview packet. These weapons will **not** be found in your competition's arsenal!

You start with **better strategy** and **superior tactics.**

You **change your focus** from getting a job to securing an interview.

You **change your focus** from getting your resume noticed in a pile of paper or e-mails to getting in front of the people who can see that you are more than a chronological resume.

You **change your focus** to acquire multiple targets of opportunity so when you are "cleared hot" and "fire for effect," you increase your chances for hitting the intended target.

CHAPTER SEVEN

Tactics for a Successful Job Search in the New Economy

You've already completed the first tactic to finding a job: You fired your resume!

TACTIC #2—TARGET COMPANIES, NOT JOBS

This is the **big** shift you need to make in your thinking! Many companies are military friendly. And depending on the state you live in, they may receive tax breaks and that puts you at an advantage over other applicants. Part of your recon is to determine which companies are military friendly. You should start by researching industries that favor military skills. These include:

- aerospace/aviation
- education
- environmental services
- finance and banking
- health care
- information technology
- logistics
- real estate
- safety
- securities and investments
- security

Some companies that favor military employees include:

- UPS
- FedEx
- Cintas

They recruit from the military because of the skills you learned while serving. You are on time, you are respectful, you will follow direction, you look sharp in their uniform, and when all hell breaks loose, you remain calm. The same applies to many companies throughout the U.S.

Instead of chasing posted jobs, start thinking about the kinds of companies you'd like to work for. Decide what geographical areas you'd like to work in and how far you're willing to commute to get to a job. Will you move? How big a company must it be? How much traveling? What kind of work environment—laid-back or button-down? Action oriented or steady? Nine-to-five or flexible, long hours? Rigid chain of command (like the police) or loose teams? What are the opportunities for advancement, benefits, etc.?

Determine all the critical factors for your life when you get a job. How flexible are you? What is important, what is "nice" versus a non-negotiable must-have? What can you compromise on? What is a deal breaker?

Then begin to research real companies of interest to you within that defined scope. At this point, as you go through this exercise, you don't care whether your targeted companies are hiring, firing, upsizing, sidewinding, or downsizing. Your goal is to find out more about the companies that fit your criteria. Whether they have jobs comes later. This is recon to know the terrain and the other side. You may never engage with them specifically but you need the intelligence.

All you know is that you'd like to go to work for any one of these companies sooner than later and if you were able to work for any one of them, you would bring added value. In other words, they could use your skills, experience, and expertise.

It's not very effective to simply respond to job postings online and wait for a call. It only makes you one of dozens (if you are lucky) but most likely hundreds who are doing the same thing with each of those postings. It is much more effective to pick one, or five, or ten companies you most want to work for, and execute a strategy to target them whether they have an appropriate opening posted or not.

Create your target list. Remember: Point of aim is point of impact. Start by searching people on LinkedIn (see Chapter 8 if you are unfamiliar with LinkedIn) in your area with titles similar to what you are looking for. What companies do they work for? Pick the ones who match your experience and criteria best.

Search LinkedIn and ask in other networks (Chambers, trade associations, Meetup, BNI, VFW, Purple Heart Association, VA, etc.) for contacts at those companies. Create your list of phone numbers and e-mail addresses for each one. You can use WhitePages.com, Jigsaw, and Google to help. Often by Googling the person's name you can find a direct phone number or e-mail address, or at least find the general format for the company e-mail addresses, then apply it to the individual's name. At the very least, you can certainly find the company's main phone number to call and ask for the person by name.

Learn what you can about those companies. Read their websites, Google them. Search for local news and announcements. Check finance sites for news about them. Check what kind of jobs they may have posted. Figure out what skills, experience, knowledge, and strengths you have that may uniquely fit their organization. **Hint:** Use the news section of the local paper or search online to see what new projects, contracts, or issues they may have that you can help solve for them.

If you're like most job seekers, you've heard about the importance of networking. So right now be prepared to spend about 15 percent or so of your time expanding your network by connecting with various people through real-world groups and social media. You are building a team to help you succeed in your mission!

Warning: As you start to network with people in your job hunt, you will soon find that some of your social contacts are looking to sell services, are other unemployed people, or multi-level/network marketing associates. You will attend events where you may find yourself surrounded by those folks "desperate for a sale" socializing with the "desperate for a job" folks. Or you'll find other vets and sit around and share "everyone loves us but no one wants to hire us" sob stories. Be aware and avoid the temptation to fall into their mindset.

Using what you've learned, create a tailored set of qualifications and **keywords** to emphasize your strengths for each organization. Write them out. Translate your military experience into the civilian equivalents!

TACTIC #3—DEFINE YOUR VALUE

Now that you've identified specific companies of interest, the next step is to determine your value to each of those companies. Take what you learned in Tactic #2 and describe your skills, experience, knowledge, and strengths that may uniquely fit their organization or solve a problem for them. Write them out. You will be using them for letters, your resume, interviews, networking, etc., with anyone in that company or industry.

Remember what we said earlier: companies don't hire you for your past; they hire you for your future; more precisely **their** future. While a strong resume and track record may be a good indicator of future performance, it does little to effectively convey the value you offer moving forward to a particular organization.

Your **value** is a blend of your **skills, experience, expertise,** and **style**. Let's take a look at each of these four components:

SKILLS

Your skills include both hard and soft skills.

Hard skills are typically learned skills. For example, we're not born with the ability to create an Excel spreadsheet; that's something we need to learn, just like driving a forklift, operating a lathe, or cooking. Hard skills typically refer to technical or administrative skills related to a company's core business.

As a veteran, some hard skills may or may not transfer to a civilian company. Let's say you've been working as a tank mechanic. You now want to go to work processing loan applications for a mortgage company in the financial services industry. In this case, your skill as a mechanic does not transfer to the mortgage company because it's not relevant to the loan processing position. However, at this stage, list **all your skills**. You will pick and choose them later depending on the needs of the target employer!

Soft skills on the other hand are almost always transferable. These skills are referred to as behavioral competencies and are often described as "people skills" or "interpersonal skills." These skills are simply how you communicate with others—be it your squad, command, clients, family, or friends—and they are crucial for success, especially in your career and business life.

Key interpersonal skills include communication, assertiveness, conflict resolution, and anger management. Good communication skills require that we listen as well as speak. We need to understand others, not just be understood ourselves. Assertiveness skills enable us to express ourselves clearly without infringing on the rights of others. Conflict is all around us all the time, so it's essential to be able to resolve differences with others in order to maintain relationships that are important to us. Finally, anger management skills allow us to vent our annoyance in an appropriate, healthy way when dealing with emergencies and solving problems that confront us on a regular basis.

EXPERIENCE

In defining the value you offer a potential employer your experience should be generally stated—generically, without reference to your former assignments, former postings, former employers, dates of employment, etc. Your experience is a key ingredient to the success you've had in previous jobs and a key element in being successful in a future job.

Experience gives you a feeling of personal growth and earns respect from others. Your career to date has been a continuous chain of experiences that have not only helped you learn, but have contributed to the value you now offer the business community and a future employer.

Military experience combined with real-world business experience is your key to success.

EXPERTISE

Your expertise refers to your specialized skill-sets, your skillfulness by virtue of possessing special knowledge. For example, being a platoon sergeant is a skill, being an aircraft crew chief with specific qualifications and training is expertise. Presently, many government agencies are downsizing on their spreadsheet, but not in body count. They are continually outsourcing tasks to cut their budgets and veterans have an upper hand when applying for those jobs that are now being outsourced.

Can you provide innovative solutions to your customers, whether internal or external? Do you thoroughly understand the products and services of your company, and more importantly, how they meet the needs of the customer? Do you add value to your company by coming up with new solutions to problems and issues related to your job?

While you may have a wide range of functional skills that you have developed over the course of your career, you may well have special or unique expertise in several areas.

STYLE

Your style is all about you as a person. It's what makes you unique.

Veterans can be challenged here. If you are straight out of the military ranks your behavior and style are very different from your civilian peers. "Yes, ma'am" and "Yes, sir" may not go over in laid-back Southern California, but they're just fine in smaller towns and the southern States. In some places your military posture, speech patterns, and mannerisms may be viewed as aggressive or aloof.

Many employers will appreciate your sacrifices, but may view you as a square peg for that round hole they are trying to fill. Unless you are willing to change your style, you may want to target companies where you will be more comfortable. That's why veterans often prefer highly regimented employers like law enforcement.

That said, how you carry yourself in terms of your sense of manners, decorum, and values gives veterans an advantage in most interviews. It's a blend of your personality and character traits such as your dependability, honesty, integrity, compassion, enthusiasm, and faith in others that make you a desirable employee for most companies—once they know how you can help them achieve their goals!

Your style is also a reflection of your attributes, such as your resourcefulness, imagination, energy, initiative, insightfulness, motivation, and intelligence. It's also how you're perceived by your peers and your superiors.

If you don't know how a company rolls—ask current employees. Ask the local vendors. Do your recon. This is important. If you are not a gregarious joiner, a job in a firm that promotes rock-and-roll events at casinos or bars is probably not a good fit. If you want to leave the regimentation behind and go back to your surfer days, a job as a police officer may not be a good choice.

TACTIC #4—TARGET THE HIRING MANAGER

Keep in mind that sending your resume into targeted companies where you'd like to go to work and where you know you would bring added value is not enough.

You need to identify the hiring manager in each of those companies. In other words, you need to identify the person who would be your potential boss. That's the one person in the organization who can truly appreciate the value you bring to the table.

How do you find the names of hiring managers in your targeted companies? This is where your professional network comes in, particularly the people you're connected with on the business-oriented social media site LinkedIn. (If you're not already on LinkedIn you need to be! It's free, and it's a fabulous tool to help you not only build and nurture a professional network, but also to gain exposure to the business community and identify targeted hiring managers. See Chapter 8 for more information on using LinkedIn).

Target veterans within LinkedIn who work for the companies you have identified as a possible employer. Join the groups in which you have a common interest. Each branch of the service has several categories. If you were part of the 101st

Airborne, then research the group and join it. After that, review what organizations you have in common. LinkedIn is the way to attain the intelligence you need to achieve your new objective.

TACTIC #5—GET REFERRED TO THE HIRING MANAGER

Without a doubt, the best way to get an interview is to be referred to the hiring manager by someone he or she trusts.

Again, this is where LinkedIn can help. Use LinkedIn to research your targeted company to find out who's working there now and who has worked there in the past. Then use your network of professionals to connect with present or former employees of your targeted company and ask for their help in identifying the hiring manager. Finally, ask your connection if you can use their name when corresponding to the hiring manager. This is what's called a warm referral.

There is also a great book called *Selling to VITO: The Very Important Top Officer* that outlines ways of getting to the decision-makers in a company. The techniques outlined in the book are real-world calls, letters, and e-mails which still are powerful tools for job seekers!

TACTIC #6—BROADCAST YOUR VALUE, NOT YOUR RESUME

We are big fans of educating the business community about who you are, and the potential value you as a veteran can offer. But educate **without** using your resume as an initial means of introduction.

Now that you've defined your value in general terms you need to convey that value to your targeted hiring managers. How?

This is where your **biography** comes into play.

In the context of job search strategy, your biography is designed to pique the interest of the reader. Customized to address a specific company and hiring manager, it's a critical component of your marketing toolbox.

Let's take a closer look at the typical characteristics of your new job hunting biography.

— One-page summary with no set format.

— Written in third-person. For example:

Ms. Jones has extensive expertise in…

She implemented a process improvement program that...
With training in medical logistics, Ms. Jones...
She has significant experience with...
Ms. Jones adds value through her unique ability to...

— Free-form with respect to content. You can include, or exclude, whatever you want.

— Refers to key competencies/transferable skills. For example:

Mr. Johnson's areas of expertise include: operations management, strategic planning and analysis, business process optimization, international operations, and large-scale project management.

— Highlights accomplishments in a generic way. For example:

Led transition of distribution and service facilities, resulting in an annual expense reduction of more than $1M.
Received "Innovator of the Year" award for 2003 and 2004.

— May or may not include references to educational background.

— Concludes with future aspirations; a forward-thinking statement of what you want to do for that company, job, or industry. For example:

Mr. Johnson is looking to establish his career with a progressive company where his significant skills, experience, and expertise in manufacturing operations can be fully utilized to increase revenue, improve the bottom line, and thereby contribute to the continued success of the organization.

Remember that your value is best conveyed by your biography, not your resume, and should be directed specifically to hiring managers in companies that are of interest to you.

In drafting your biography, pretend that one of those hiring managers has asked you the question:

"How can you help our company?"

The answer you give, which should include a blend of your skills, experience, expertise, and style, is what goes down on paper and becomes your biography. Then flip it around to third person. Your biography characterizes the value you offer moving forward, while your resume is nothing more than a track record of past positions, postings, and employment.

From the employer's perspective your value always trumps your resume. This is the veteran's "golden nugget." You are creating a description of yourself and your accomplishments based on the skills you learned in the military. When you draft a resume, you are trying to figure out too many things at multiple times and ways. The biography is just like asking you the typical interview question, "Tell me about yourself." And I can guarantee you that will be asked this question in one form or another. This helps the reader know the answers!

TACTIC #7—INITIATE A DIALOG

Depending on the situation, there are two cover letters that accompany your biography when introducing yourself directly to a hiring manager:

The **Strategic Value letter** and the
Strategic Job Listing letter

Samples of these two letters can be found in Chapter 3 of this book.

THE STRATEGIC VALUE LETTER

The **Strategic Value letter** is sent to a hiring manager in a company where there are no apparent openings at all. In this scenario all you are aiming to do is to introduce yourself to the hiring manager, with your bio, to give him/her a teaser of your background. As the letter states, you are not looking for a job.

You then follow up several days later with a phone call to answer any questions he or she may have about your background and to restate your confidence that at some point in the future you could bring added value to the company. Then ask if you can stay in touch, perhaps connecting once a month or so through e-mail or LinkedIn, so that "should an opportunity open up in the future where I could bring added-value perhaps we could get together and talk about it."

When you make your follow-up call to the hiring manager, several days after mailing your biography and cover letter, you'll experience one of several scenarios:

Follow-Up Call to Strategic Value Letter

If you get sent to voice mail, leave a brief message and give a time window to let the manager know when you will be calling again. Invite the manager to call you and leave your phone number, for example:

"Hello Mr. Jones. This is John Smith calling and I'm following up on some information I forwarded to you several days ago. I'm sorry I missed you; however I will try again tomorrow between 9 a.m. and noon. In the meantime, if you have the opportunity to call me I can be reached at (555) 555-5555. I look forward to speaking with you."

If you're fortunate enough to be connected directly to the hiring manager, the typical conversation may be:

"Hi John, I got your information and looked at your background. There's nothing for you here. Sorry, I can't help you."

Instead of saying "thank you" and hanging up, your response should be something like this:

"I understand Mr. Jones, and I appreciate you taking my call anyway. As I mentioned in my letter I certainly didn't expect there to be any opportunities for me at the moment. I simply wanted to take a couple of minutes to introduce myself to you, give you an overview of my background, and to let you know that I'm confident that at some point in the future I could bring added value to you and your company. Would it be okay if I could stay in touch with you, perhaps sending you an e-mail once a month or so or staying connected through LinkedIn, so that should something open up in the future perhaps we could sit down and talk about it?"

Nine times out of ten the hiring manager will say yes to you staying in touch. Once in awhile you'll get someone who tells you to get the heck out of his life, but you wouldn't want to go to work there anyway.

On the other hand, you may have a meaningful conversation about your background and the potential value you offer. The hiring manager may even ask for your resume. At this point this is the best outcome since it appears there is genuine interest. Now you know your resume is going directly to the hiring manager, the one person who can truly appreciate what you can potentially bring to the table, and your resume will get the attention it deserves.

Follow-up E-mail

After talking with your target, it is prudent to send a periodic e-mail. **Do not start** the process with an e-mail. Only send an e-mail when you have permission from the recipient! Otherwise, it could be considered spam.

So let's say you have successfully had a real conversation but no opportunities may exist at the moment. At least you've established a good dialog with the hiring manager and a very valid reason to stay in touch by sending a simple e-mail once a month or so, for example:

Good morning Mr. Jones,

You may remember we spoke a month or so ago about my background in project management and my interest in your company. I just wanted to let you know that I enjoy staying in touch. Please let me know if there is anything I can do to help you moving forward.

All the best, John Smith

You want to use any excuse you can find to send the hiring manager an e-mail. Here is a potential example:

Hi Mr. Jones,

You may remember we spoke a month or so ago about my background in project management and my interest in your company. I noticed last week's article in the Business Journal *about your recent growth and third-quarter earnings which were above expectations. Congratulations. Please let me know if there is anything I can do to help you moving forward.*

All the best, John Smith.

THE STRATEGIC JOB LISTING LETTER

The **Strategic Job Listing letter** is used when you are responding to a specific job posting.

In this scenario you send your resume and standard cover letter to HR, as requested in the job posting, but at the same time see if you can identify the hiring manager who would oversee that position. Then you send your biography and this letter directly to him/her, with a follow-up phone call to set up a meeting. Don't send your resume to the hiring manager since it will just be forwarded on to HR.

With this approach, when you make your follow-up telephone call to the hiring manager you'll experience one of two typical scenarios:

Success Tip: Use a clear phone line, preferably a land line, to minimize static or the call being dropped.

Telephone Follow-Up

If you get voice mail, leave a brief message and give a time window to let the manager know when you will be calling again. Invite the manager to call you and leave your phone number. For example:

> *Hello, Ms. Williams. This is John Smith calling and I'm following up on some information I forwarded to you several days ago with regard to my qualifications for the senior project manager position. I'm sorry I missed you, however I will try again tomorrow between 9 a.m. and noon. In the meantime, if you have the opportunity to call me I can be reached at (555) 555-5555. I look forward to speaking with you.*

If you're fortunate enough to be connected directly to the hiring manager, your conversation could begin with:

Hello, Ms. Williams. This is John Smith calling and I'm following up on some information I forwarded to you several days ago with regard to my qualifications for the senior project manager position. As I mentioned in my letter, I have forwarded my resume directly to your human resources department however, as you and I both know it's probably buried in a stack a foot high. My concern is that my value is buried in that stack and that's why I'm contacting you directly.

When you forward your biography and cover letter to your targeted hiring managers **don't use e-mail**. A busy manager gets a hundred e-mails a day and with a simple click of the mouse you're gone, along with your potential value.

Instead, go to the post office and send your biography and cover letter by Priority Mail. In two to three days it will arrive in a flat, red-white-and-blue Priority Mail envelope that will create a sense of urgency. Odds are it will be placed right on the hiring manager's desk. It will cost you a few dollars but well worth it. Remember, the goal is to get noticed by the right person and Priority Mail should help!

Regardless of whether you're using the Strategic Value letter or the Strategic Job Listing letter be sure to manage your activity in terms of following up as indicated in your correspondence. The key is to follow up promptly so your information is still fresh in the hiring manager's mind.

THE BIOGRAPHY

When properly used, your biography offers six distinct advantages over your resume:

1. With your biography you can promote yourself any way you want. Remember, your resume is very restrictive in its format. You have to include where you worked, how long you worked there, what you did, how long you did it, and your educational background. With your resume there's no way to avoid providing that information.

2. Your biography avoids the pitfalls of the resume format. Resumes are typically presented in chronological format, functional format, or a combination of both. The entire document is related to the past and you are severely limited in how you can present yourself.

3. You can customize your selling approach to prospective employers **before** submitting a resume. This is a huge advantage because with your biography you can address specific areas where you can add value to a particular

organization moving forward, whereas your resume is nothing more than a reflection of the past.

4. Your biography avoids HR department personnel completely. Since it's sent directly to key decision-makers, your biography never goes anywhere near human resources. They wouldn't know what to do with it anyway since it doesn't look like a resume.

5. Your biography has more credibility. Your approach with your biography is more believable since it's tailored to a specific situation or company. Your resume is just a track record of employment.

   And, most importantly…

6. Your biography differentiates you from 99 percent of all other job seekers. While others are relying on a powerful resume and knock-'em-dead cover letter to get them noticed by some personnel jockey, you're working smarter, not harder. You're making an end run around the masses and differentiating yourself by targeting the hiring manager—the one person who can truly appreciate the potential value you offer. You're standing out from the crowd!

Effective Use of your Biography

You can use your biography in a variety of different ways:

- Personal networking—updating friends and relatives about your background while informing them of your career transition.
- Professional networking—staying connected, or reconnecting, with former coworkers and people you meet at various networking groups, industry associations, etc., during and after your job search.
- Targeting companies—the most effective way to educate the business community and get the attention of hiring managers in companies of interest.

CHAPTER EIGHT

Using Social Networks in Your Job Hunt

Remember that your biggest challenge in your job search is differentiation. How do you separate yourself from all other job seekers in a highly competitive job market?

As a veteran, you have an advantage that only 1 percent of job applicants will have. Be proud of that fact and use it to your tactical advantage.

As you continue to encounter the challenges of career transition, increase your odds by creating your own unique identity in the job market.

You must become a unique brand.

This nontraditional approach will help separate you from your competition but it requires some hard work. As a military veteran, hard work should be something you understand. Your training should give you an unfair advantage because you understand the objective and now have some of the tactics you need to achieve that objective.

Use your biography to convey the value you represent to the business community. With this approach you'll be **creating opportunity** instead of spending the majority of your time chasing posted jobs and just **waiting for opportunity**.

An essential tactic in your new strategy to market yourself instead of your resume is to use the social networking tool LinkedIn.

AN INTRODUCTION TO LINKEDIN

LinkedIn is a social network designed for business professionals. Its name tells what it was designed for—linking professionals with each other. Think of Facebook as a family picnic where you catch up with friends and family, while LinkedIn is more like a business chamber mixer. Members expect to do business with other members and help find qualified job applicants.

This business-like mentality is important to keep in mind when creating your LinkedIn profile, adding updates, seeking introductions to new contacts, joining

LinkedIn groups (a very powerful resource) and so on. Rather than offer cutesy games and tons of spam, LinkedIn is geared specifically to professionals as a source of information and introductions.

Most Fortune 500 executives are on LinkedIn. There are also company profiles to help you do research on the company's locations, officers, size, and especially anyone you know inside! Used properly, LinkedIn is a job seeker's best resource.

CREATING YOUR LINKEDIN PROFILE

Signing up for and using basic LinkedIn is free to users. The site does have some advertising, but it's unobtrusive and often job related. All you need to get started is to go to http://www.LinkedIn.com and create a LinkedIn login to sign up for a free account.

Once you sign up for a LinkedIn account, you can create your own professional profile. Your photograph (also known as your avatar) should be a clear and compelling head shot and not the funky chicken costume you wore for Halloween. It will pay to have a good professional photographer do a series of photographs for your social media needs!

This profile is your chance to post your **biography**! You explain who you are and what you offer to other members of the LinkedIn community. Use keywords to describe who you are and what you can do for your target industries or companies. For your reference, here's an example of my LinkedIn profile which showcases both my military experience and my civilian employee value.

Tom Stein

President GreyHawk Aviation Safety

Certifications

SDVOSB, Service Disabled Veteran Owned Small Business
CAGE/NCAGE: 6KBY4 License CA 125257

Certified Career Management Professional (CCMP)
Institute of Career Certification International (ICCI) January 2013

Summary

Thomas Stein has more than 20 years of broad-based experience in senior executive operational management, program, and project management, and education. Within the aviation arena he has managed implementations of newly introduced aircraft prototypes and technical systems. In a Fortune 50 company, he established the first successful Business Continuity Program and IT Program Development Methodology.

Prior to entering corporate America, Mr. Stein was a Senior Marine Officer specializing in the subject areas of Aviation, Information Technology, Logistics, Operational Threat Analysis, and World Wide Contingency Planning.

Tom is also an Assistant Professor for Embry-Riddle Aeronautical University and a member of the faculty staff since 1998. He instructs and develops programs for undergraduate and graduate students.

His passion to help people and especially veterans continues and in 2011 and 2012 he co-authored a series of 6 books focusing on Military transition and careers called TheHireTactics. In January 2013 Tom attained his cerification as a Career Management Professional from the Institute of Career Certification International (ICCI: http://www.careercertification.org/index.html)..

In June of 2012, Mr. Stein accepted the position of Chairman of the Board for the Orange County Veteran Employment Committee (OCVEC).

A graduate of the Naval Academy, Mr. Stein holds numerous degrees and certificates in Aviation, Education, and Information Technology.

Page1

Publications

Thesis: ANALYSIS OF AVIATION MISHAPS USING CURRENT AVIATION FORENSICS METHODOLOGIES AND EXHIBITING HUMAN ERROR AS THE PRIMARY ROOT CAUSE

Embry Riddle University September 27, 2011

Authors: Tom S.

The aviation industry as a whole partitions the root cause of aviation accidents into specific areas when in fact all accidents are attributed to human error. Causes are grouped into the areas of pilot error, weather, maintenance, air traffic control, and the airframe itself. This exercise of grouping is misleading and incorrect. Additionally, the industry collects and segregates other causal factors while segregating additional contributors deemed as contributors, like terrorism. This retrospective analysis examines aviation commercial and non commercial mishaps picked randomly, reviewed, and diagnosed for their true root cause. Analysis will indicate causal factors should not be segmented into specific area such as weather and be focused on human activities within the aviation industry. Furthermore, the work will exhibit all mishaps are caused by human error and recommend new categorization to facilitate better investigation techniques and improved education to the aviation industry

Book 1: Veteran Employment Tactics - Packaging Yourself for Job Hunting Success

February 23, 2012

Authors: Tom S., Gregory S. W.

"VETERAN EMPLOYMENT TACTICS! – Packaging Yourself for Job Hunting Success" is the first book in TheHireTactics™ series and introduces military veterans to the tools you need to brand yourself to ensure you separate yourself from your competition. In this book, you will learn how the job search system really works and how to use your tactical advantage as a military veteran!

The authors will share how to develop and use a proven strategic approach for your job search instead of the "traditional" resume-based approach. Using this new approach and new tools will help shorten your time in job transition. This series is for job seekers who are frustrated, discouraged and increasingly fed up and want answers and solutions and not clever book titles and unrealistic promises.

TheHireChallenge™ books are deliberately designed to be short and easy-to-read. I want to show you why you are probably NOT successful in your job search and give you the tools to succeed.

Book 2: Fire Your Resume - Military Edition

February 23, 2012

Authors: Tom S., Gregory S. Wood, CCMP

Your job search using a traditional resume and cover letter is simply NOT working in today's competitive job market. Job hunting can be extra challenging for military veterans because the employer will probably be in the 99% who did not serve and do not understand what benefits a veteran brings to their workplace.

In this tough economy, our Vets need special strategies and tactics for finding civilian employment that takes full advantage of their skills, experience and expertise. Authors Tom Stein (retired USMC) and Greg Wood (Certified Career Management Professional) share the ugly truth that Human Resources Departments are, without doubt, your biggest obstacle to finding your next job. Learn how to outflank HR by going beyond

Page2

your resume and broadcasting your value directly to hiring managers in the business community. Book includes sample letters and scripts

Get the intel and tools you need for your job hunting mission! Written specifically to help veterans take the skills they learned in the military and turn them into an advantage in their job search.

Book 3: Lock and Load! - 24 Job Interview Questions Military Veterans Must Know
February 23, 2012
Authors: Tom S.

Being asked to take an interview means you are 80% of the way to accomplishing your mission. The interview is where you "seal the deal" and preparation is the key to success! In the third book in TheHireTactics™ series you'll learn how to demonstrate the value you bring to the table by conducting a tactical and strategic interview that will greatly enhance your chances of winning the job offer. Additional question general to all job interviews can be found in Greg Wood's book, "Nailed It!" But just like basic training, you need to learn and practice your skills for this critical part of the job search process! You MUST rehearse your interview answers.

Book 4: PAY DAY! - Negotiating Your True Worth, Not a Salary
February 23, 2012
Authors: Tom S., Gregory S. W.

Let's face it, military veterans are not used to negotiating their pay! A table from the Pentagon listing your rank and time in service pretty much sets your paycheck and benefits. In this fourth book in TheHireTactics™ series, you'll learn how to evaluate whether or not a job is worth taking and then how to negotiate the difference between what you're offered and your true worth to the organization. Transitioning military have to be very careful to understand there is a difference between what you need to survive and what you deserve or want. Military veterans, who lack knowledge and experience in how salaries are set, and what bonuses should be offered, can be taken advantage of. This book is your guide to salary success!

TheHireTactics™
April 27, 2012
Authors: Tom S., Gregory S. W.

Welcome to TheHireTactics™, the best-selling series dedicated to helping military veterans succeed in their job search mission. This eBook combines the original four books in the series: Book One – "VETERAN EMPLOYMENT TACTICS! – Packaging Yourself for Job Hunting Success; Book Two – "FIRE YOUR RESUME! – Tactics for a Successful Job Search in the New Economy" ; Book Three – "LOCK AND LOAD! – 24 Job Interview Questions Military Veterans Need to Know!"; and Book Four – "PAY DAY! – Negotiating Your True Worth, Not Just a Salary". The books offer veterans just leaving the service as well as those with civilian experience the tips, tactics and strategies they need to successfully find employment in this challenging economy.

Page3

Skills & Expertise

Published Author
Aviation
Operations Management
IT Management
Logistics
Program Management
Process Improvement
Emergency Management
Organizational Leadership
Leadership Development
Team Leadership
Team Building
Mentoring
Coaching
Education Management
Adult Education
Government
Military
Public Speaking

Experience

Chairman of the Board, Orange County Veterans Employment Committee (OCVEC). at Orange County Veterans Employment Committee

June 2012 - Present (1 year 2 months)

Orange County Veterans Employment Committee (OCVEC).
http://www.occalveteransemploymentcommittee.org/

Our mission is to connect local veterans with the resources and services they need for civilian employment and encourage strong partnerships in our community to promote their hiring.

President at GreyHawk Aviation Safety

2006 - Present (7 years)

GreyHawk Enterprises is a Service Disabled Veteran Owned Small Business (SDVOSB).

We focus on advisement, training, and education in the areas of aviation safety.

Assistant Professor, Aerospace Sciences at Embry-Riddle Aeronautical University

May 1998 - Present (15 years 3 months)

Assistant Professor for #1 rated Aerospace Undergraduate University in the world. Areas of specialization address the aerospace industry ranging from Aviation Crash Investigation and Safety to Systems Engineering, Project and Program Management.

Board Member & Treasurer at Orange County Veterans Employment Committee (OCVEC).

Page4

February 2011 - June 2012 (1 year 5 months)

Board Member: Orange County Veterans Employment Committee (OCVEC).

We connect local Veterans to resources and services for reemployment and encourage strong partnerships in our community to promote the hiring of Veterans.

College Vice President at WyoTech
April 2011 - September 2011 (6 months)

WyoTech, formerly known as Wyoming Technical Institute, is dedicated to high-quality, college-level, career-oriented education in the automotive, diesel, motorcycle, HVAC, watercraft, and collision/refinishing industries. Each WyoTech program is designed to provide our students with the skills they need to achieve their education goals.

Military Affairs and Training, Floating Campus President at WyoTech
January 2010 - April 2011 (1 year 4 months)

WyoTech, formerly known as Wyoming Technical Institute, is dedicated to high-quality, college-level, career-oriented education in the automotive, diesel, motorcycle, HVAC, watercraft, and collision/refinishing industries. Each WyoTech program is designed to provide our students with the skills they need to achieve their education goals.

Senior Manager, Programs: IS and BCP Programs at Ingram Micro
February 2001 - January 2010 (9 years)

Ingram Micro, Inc. NYSE: IM is a Fortune 100 company founded in 1979 as Micro D and based in Santa Ana, California. It is the world's largest technology distributor and a leading technology sales, marketing and logistics company. The company distributes and markets IT products from computer hardware suppliers, networking equipment suppliers, and software publishers worldwide.

Marine Corps Officer at U.S. Marine Corps
1980 - 2000 (20 years)

Mr. Stein was a Lieutenant Colonel in the Marine Corps specializing in the subject areas of Aviation, Logistics, and Information Technology. As a program manager he has held some of the highest achievable positions and designations in his fields of expertise.

2 recommendations available upon request

Education

Embry-Riddle Aeronautical University
MS, Aeronautical Science, 2008 - 2011

Naval Postgraduate School
MS, Information Systems, 1990 - 1992

United States Naval Academy

Page5

BS, Resources Management & Naval Sciences, 1976 - 1980
Activities and Societies: Commandant's List, Varsity Sprint Football, Military Jump Club

---

Honors and Awards

Mr. Stein has received numerous awards over the years:

• As a top performer, he has been selected and awarded two scholarships for graduate studies in Information Systems (1990) and Aerospace Science (2005).
• In 1995 he received recognition by President Clinton for software development in the areas of human resources and IT application development.
• In 1997 and 2001 he received additional recognition for his outstanding performance in aviation and logistic program management.
• He received a 2004 Award of Excellence from Ingram Micro for Sarbanes-Oxley compliance efforts in relation to mainframe access security.
• He received a 2005 Award of Excellence from Ingram Micro for MicroSoft Compliance Initiatives.
• In 2007 he received an Exceptional Performance Award from Ingram Micro.

Page6

Tom Stein

President GreyHawk Aviation Safety

2 people have recommended Tom

"Tom Stein is one of the most conscientious, diligent human beings I have ever encountered in my 37 year professional career as an aviator and military analyst. A consummate professional, Tom demands the very best of himself and those around him. His abilities as a leader, teacher, and problem solver are unsurpassed. Tom infuses an inspirational demeanor into every project that he is involved in producing positive outcomes with on-time and under budget deliverables. Direct, efficient, and effective, he cuts to the chase in defining and solving any problem with a variety of tools attained during an exemplary career often characterized by formidable challenge and a frenetic pace."

— **Bill M.**, *Pilot, United States Marine Corps*, worked directly with Tom at U.S. Marine Corps

"I've known Tom for 25 years. His leadership skills, values and integrity are what you would expect from a Marine. I mean that with the highest respect."

— **Mark C.**, *Owner, Bill's Sweeping Service, Inc.*, was with another company when working with Tom at U.S. Marine Corps

Contact Tom on LinkedIn

Page7

Remember, since this is a professionally-oriented website, it's important that information in your profile represents your business or working side. LinkedIn is not the place to share cute baby photos or show how drunk you got at last week's party. My social media advisors recommend you review the profile of other members in your industry to see how they structure their descriptions.

Some of the things you can add to a profile include the basics of your resume, a summary about yourself, your contact information, links to your website and/or blog, your Twitter account, and more.

Once your profile is ready, you publish it and start looking for connections. A connection is a person that you know or would like to know more about on LinkedIn. Essentially the idea is to create as many direct connections as you can by adding people within your own professional circle and branching out to include their connections. Do not connect to people you do not know directly. You can get penalized for doing that too many times.

Your connections can also provide introductions to other professionals you might be interested in meeting. Connections can also provide you with standing recommendations for employment.

Success Tip: Do **not** invite all your contacts to be your LinkedIn friend at one time! Ignore the offer to import all your contacts when you first set up your LinkedIn account. Choose the individuals for whom LinkedIn fits their needs and profile. Then invite them individually with a **personalized** invitation. Explain why you think it is a good idea they link to you.

HOW LINKEDIN CAN HELP YOU

LinkedIn allows you to:

- Get online recommendations for your professional abilities and your character.
- Get introductions to potential employers or colleagues in your field.
- Search for military-friendly organizations.
- Search available job postings placed on the LinkedIn website by members and member companies. You can search by job type, location, or company name.

While you can also search the web for jobs through LinkedIn, the big benefit is that many job posts are exclusive to LinkedIn and aren't advertised elsewhere. In addition, there is a chance that someone within your LinkedIn network already works there or knows someone who does, giving you a big foot in the door for an interview.

One way to accelerate your link building is to join various groups that align with your interests and participate in discussions. Having a group in common with another LinkedIn user is one way you can invite others into your network. Each group discussion contains its own job listings. Be helpful to other group members and **don't sell**. Ask for help and offer help.

You can create an online resume that mirrors your paper resume. LinkedIn allows hiring companies and recruiters to search for professionals who might fit their criteria. The secret to resume success on LinkedIn is knowing the common keywords for job candidates in that field. You learn those by reviewing job descriptions and the company profiles posted on LinkedIn.

SECTION 3

Lock and Load!

INTRODUCTION

So you've gotten past the HR sensors. You've successfully networked your biography onto a hiring manager's desk. It's now time to impress your future employer face-to-face. My coauthor Greg Wood is an expert in nailing the job interview. He created a unique in-home job search system that provides you with direction for success in your job transition. One of the most popular parts of TheHireRoad™ is the collection of 69 interview questions you are likely to be asked during a job interview as well as 15 questions you should consider asking the interviewer in return. Job seekers use these questions to prepare and rehearse for the interview where they will hopefully seal the deal and be offered a job.

As a military veteran in career transition—either from active military or from one civilian position to another—you have unique skills and unique challenges. Your unique skills and training give you an advantage but **only** if properly presented to your future employers.

Just like basic training, you need to learn and practice your skills for this critical part of the job search process! You **must** rehearse your interview answers.

As you begin to prepare for your upcoming interview, remember that you have a choice. This is the **same** choice you had when you began your job search. You can follow the traditional approach, which is **reactive**, or you can choose to differentiate yourself by being **strategically proactive.**

Why is this difference important? Let me take a minute to talk about interviewing from both a traditional and strategic perspective.

Think about the reason you've been selected to come in and interview. It's not because you're a nice person who's out of work and needs a paycheck. It's because the hiring manager has problems and issues that need to be solved. By solving those problems, the hiring manager looks good, the department looks good, and profitability will be enhanced. The hiring manager has looked at your background, has determined that you represent a solution to his problems, and wants to consider hiring you. Your employment is all about solving problems.

When you're invited in to interview it's important to remember that you're 80 percent of the way there. The hiring manager knows you can do the job, it's right there on your resume. However, if you're one of five candidates interviewing for the same job, you **all** represent solutions to the problems at hand.

The manager's challenge is to determine who is the best fit. It's this remaining 20 percent, this fit, that will drive his or her decision to select one candidate over another. Are you going to be able to work well with your new boss and a new team? And are you the type of person who will mesh with the culture and environment of the company?

> *YOUR challenge is to convince the hiring manager that YOU are the BEST fit and her best candidate, that you are her PREFERRED SOLUTION to her employee hiring problem.*

The vast majority of job seekers go into a traditional interview with two key emotions: anxiety and fear. They suffer from anxiety because they don't know what questions are going to be asked and if they can answer them in a professional way. They also have a fear of rejection. They know they're competing with others for the same job and they want to be the one chosen. Their whole approach is reactive. They nervously clutch their resume with beads of sweat forming on their forehead, wait for the same questions that the hiring manager asks of each candidate, and rely on their past experience to get them the job. They fail to connect with the interviewer, fail to achieve differentiation, and therefore look like every other candidate.

The chemistry you're able to establish between you and the hiring manager is essential in moving the process forward to an offer. And that chemistry begins the moment you walk in the manager's office. It's here where your choice to conduct a proactive and strategic interview will differentiate you from your competition.

As you begin thinking about your upcoming interview, keep in mind three important points about hiring managers:

First, the odds are that the hiring manager interviewing you is one of the 99 percent of civilians who has not served in the military.

Second, the majority of hiring managers dislike interviewing. They would rather get back to their regular job.

Third, the vast majority of hiring managers don't have a clue about how to conduct an effective interview. Why? Because they haven't been trained. Many make their hiring decisions based on a popularity contest, rather than choosing the candidate who can best solve the problems and issues that will help increase profitability.

The purpose of the interview, from both your perspective and that of the hiring manager, should be a discussion of the work at hand. However, since most hiring managers are poorly prepared they conduct nothing more than standard interrogations, asking the same questions of each candidate.

Even though you're going be conducting a strategic interview and taking subtle control, you will still be quizzed about a variety of topics unrelated to the job.

The following 24 sample questions here will help prepare you for your forthcoming business meeting or interview. In addition to my discussion of each, I've included suggested responses.

Obviously these are not intended to be pat answers since each reply you give has to be unique to you, your experience, your situation, and the job you're interviewing for. Also, they will not be asked in any order or with these exact same words. This is to teach you how to answer the most common questions.

You may want to record the questions and your answers and the listen to them. You may also want to create flashcards with the questions and your potential answers and randomly pick one to answer periodically until you can easily and smoothly answer the questions.

We have also left room at the bottom of each page for you to write down any thoughts you have when reading the question and your personal answers.

CHAPTER NINE

24 Job Interview Questions Military Veterans Must Know!

QUESTION 1: Tell me about yourself. . .

This is often asked at the outset of the interview to help put you at ease. It's where you begin to connect with the hiring manager, establishing the chemistry that's so important to your successful interview. If you're not prepared, this question may make you quite uncomfortable. However, I believe it can be of significant benefit to you because it's a great opportunity to convey some important points prior to the nitty-gritty of the interview. Since this is an open-ended question, you want to be careful not to ramble on, so I suggest limiting your response to no more than maybe a minute or minute and a half.

In order to connect on the same level with the hiring manager, the first thing you must do is to clarify which direction to go, providing either personal or professional information. So when you hear "tell me about yourself," you'll want to begin your reply by asking:

"Do you mean on a personal basis or professional basis? Is there something in particular you'd like me to focus on?"

The answer you get will give you the direction to follow. While most hiring managers will be interested in your professional background, occasionally the interest will be personal, or it could be both. Let the interviewer tell you what he or she is looking for!

Note: You need to be careful as to what personal information you disclose. Prospective employers have limits on what they are permitted to ask you. So many now rely on you volunteering sensitive information when asked an open-ended question like this one. For example, if you are a female, your plans for a family are not relevant in a job interview. We recommend sticking to where you were born, raised, went to high school, and if applicable where you went to college. You can then add some basic information on where and when you enlisted and some of your duty stations.

As you continue, you'll want to touch on four key components in your response. The first is to state your functional expertise in present tense. Remember, your expertise is current, and didn't end when you left the service or your last employer.

We have provided a quick reference guide to the equivalents in most companies for the various military ranks. These are just guidelines.

Military Rank	Civilian Comparison
E1 through E3	Systems Analyst/Junior Associate
E4 through E5	Manager
E6 and E7	Mid Level to Senior Manager
E8 and E9	Junior Executive/Executive
01 through 03	Manager/Sr Manager/Jr Executive
04 and 05	Senior Executive
06 and above	COO/CIO/CFO/CEO Equivalents

For example:

> *"I* ***am*** *a mid-level manager (sergeant/staff sergeant/gunnery sergeant) serving in the (Army, Air Force, Marine Corps, Navy, Coast Guard, etc.), or "I am a senior executive, senior manager (E7/E8 or 04/05) having recently served in the (Army, Air Force, Marine Corps, Navy, etc.)."*

Being a leader and a manager is not the same thing; however they are necessarily linked and complementary. The **manager's** job is to plan, organize and coordinate. The **leader's** job is to inspire and motivate. This is an important distinction that you must understand prior to going out and engaging your newly acquired targets of opportunity.

This leads to the second component, which is a brief summary of your career. This summary is not a recitation of your resume but a narrative that provides the hiring manager with an overview. For example:

> *"My background includes more than 10 years experience in the telecommunications industry. But let me take a step back and tell you how I got to where I am today."*

As you briefly describe your career, try to mention one or two accomplishments by telling a story that highlights your strengths.

If you were an enlisted E-1 through E-9 make sure you include any college or certificates you received. Many civilians will assume that non-officer grade personnel do not have degrees or specialty training.

Remember you are talking to a civilian. If you start discussing military operations within the battalion or regiment, you may drive a wedge of misunderstanding between you and the hiring manager and could lose the job.

After bringing the hiring manager back up to present day, this now allows you to lead right into the third component, which is the reason you left your last employer. This issue is now on the table and resolved. For example:

> *"The reason I'm no longer with the (Army, Air Force, Marine Corps, Navy, Coast Guard, etc.) is I fulfilled my military obligations and I'm eager to start a new career."*

It's just that simple to say.

The final component is what we call "painting a picture." You conclude your response by stating what you're looking to do moving forward. For example:

> *"What I'm looking to do now is to join a progressive company that will take full advantage of my project management skills. I want to work at an organization where I can continue to grow professionally for the long term, make a substantial contribution to the success of the company, and be fairly compensated for my efforts. I'm hoping that's the kind of opportunity that we'll be discussing today."*

QUESTION 2: Why are you no longer in the service?

When explaining why you're no longer with your former "employer" or the service, always tell the truth and give the same reason you gave to people who are references and to other companies. Don't take the chance that people in your network may provide conflicting information.

There can be many legitimate reasons why you left your former employer or the service. These could include downsizing due to economic conditions, a restructuring, outsourcing of job functions, relocation of the company itself, a merger or acquisition, or the company going out of business. Be truthful, but don't go overboard. Too much information can lead to conversations that will distract the hiring manager.

Whatever the reason, avoid using the words "terminated" or "fired" or any other words that have a negative connotation. If you were being coaxed out of your company and given the option to resign, then resignation was the reason for leaving.

Here are some sample responses that may apply to your situation:

"It's simply time to move on. The service was a great experience which I will never regret."

OR . . .

"The reason I'm no longer with the service is I fulfilled my military obligations and I'm eager to start a new career using the skills I acquired which would be of benefit to your company."

OR . . .

"I'm sure you have read about the military downsizing taking place. The service underwent a major restructuring and my position was eliminated."

OR . . .

"I wanted to stay in this area after I fulfilled my obligation but they wanted to transfer me out of the area. I decide not to accept the offer."

Note: This is a risky response when you are talking with a company with multiple locations where transfers are a real possibility. This is best used for smaller, local-only companies who are proud of their roots in the area.

____

____

____

____

QUESTION 3: Why are you thinking of leaving the service?

If your resume reflects current employment, meaning that you are still on active duty or in the reserves, anticipate this question being asked and prepare your response carefully. Make sure you tell the truth and give the same reason you gave to others. Don't take the chance that people in your network may provide conflicting information. There could be a number of legitimate reasons why you may be thinking of leaving the service.

Here are a few suggested responses that may apply to your situation:

"I do not wish to go and leave my family for 13 months again. I've already done it twice."

OR . . .

"I want to start working soon and also take advantage of my benefits and start college/school. In the service we were gone so much that you really did not have the time to do those things."

OR . . .

"My fiancé and I want to get married soon and going back overseas was not an option at this time."

OR . . .

"While I really enjoy being in the service, my spouse has been transferred to another state."

While you may actually be thinking of leaving your job because you're bored stiff, you can't stand your manager, or you don't enjoy the 13-month deployments, make sure that whatever reason you give does not have a negative tone. The examples I just gave are neutral and can fit many situations.

____

____

____

____

____

____

QUESTION 4: Why do you want to come to work for our company?

This is the **big-opportunity-to-score-points question!** And this is the one most job seekers blow, big time. They have shotgunned resumes everywhere and did little to no preparation for the interview. They know nothing about the company and maybe a little about the industry.

This question allows you to respond in a way that shows you've done your research. This question can set you apart from all the other applicants so do your pre-interview preparation!

Mention two or three positive aspects about the company that appeal to you. For example, the industry they're in, the company's innovative products, or their history of growth. You can also refer to information you discovered about the job itself, the culture of the company and how such an environment would allow you to maximize your contribution.

Your response could be:

> *"I'm interested in [name of company] for several reasons. Not only do you have an impressive history of growth in the industry over the last few years, but you're also developing leading-edge products which represent a potential increase in market share. My research has also identified several challenges that you're currently facing; challenges where my skills, experience and expertise could be of significant value. I feel that joining your company would be to our mutual benefit."*

____

____

____

QUESTION 5: What professional accomplishments were you most proud of when you were in the service?

Don't say you earned several Good Conduct Medals. The hiring manager is going to be lost. They expect you to conduct yourself at all times as a professional or they may equate Good Conduct Medals to their son's Cub Scout Merit Badge! Both equally give the wrong picture. The same goes for Achievement or Meritorious Service Medals you may have received in the military. These are great awards, but civilians who have never served will not appreciate their significance.

You want to refer to specific job-related accomplishments on your resume. Choose those accomplishments that relate, in some way, to the job you're applying for. Explain how the experiences you've gained through these accomplishments enable you to face similar situations in the future.

For example, if you're applying for a senior project/program manager position, your response may be:

> *"One of my proudest accomplishments was when I was in the service. I was recognized for superior performance in a very high pressure situation. We were in tough working environment, working very long hours, and my bosses recognized that my team never missed a task or had any major hiccups. I received a promotion within a month (meaning you were meritoriously promoted). Up until that time, I had only managed smaller working groups/units."*

QUESTION 6: What do you consider your major strengths?

This question is almost always asked during the interview along with the weakness question. Aside from mentioning the obvious, such as your interpersonal skills, talk about your strengths as they relate to the job you're currently interviewing for. This is where having a job description of the position(s) before the interview is imperative. You **must** respond in a way that shows them you are qualified for the job.

Focus your strengths on those that are reflected in the description. Finish your response with:

> *"I'm convinced I have the talent to fill this position, I'm driven to accomplish any task. I believe this is a great fit, not only for me professionally but also for your organization."*

____

____

____

____

QUESTION 7: What do you consider your greatest weakness?

This question is almost always asked by the hiring manager and, for some reason, is one of the most feared by the candidate. But it doesn't have to be if you're prepared. In my opinion, it's one of the top five dumb questions that can be asked in an interview.

Why?

Because it has nothing to do with the problems and issues faced by the hiring manager. The manager's not interested in your actual weaknesses, but how you respond to the question. What's important to note is that they can see right through standard responses, such as:

> *"I'm a perfectionist"* or *"I'm a workaholic and tend to spend too much time at the office."*

So skip the obvious answers and be more tactical!

Whatever weakness you choose, make sure that you put a positive spin on it. An easy way to remember how best to respond is the Oreo cookie example. The dark cookie on top is a positive statement about you, the white filling is your perceived weakness, and the dark cookie on the bottom is another positive statement.

For example:

> *"Well, throughout my time in the service, many times I worked in a team environment. I'm very committed, and I like to see all tasks completed in a timely manner that satisfy the requirements. I have to tell you though; sometimes I get very frustrated with other team members who tend to drag their feet and don't share that same kind of commitment. I like working with people who are highly motivated like me and share a common pursuit of excellence in their work."*

In this response, you began by mentioning one of your strengths—how committed you are to your work (the dark cookie on top). You then mentioned your perceived weakness—your frustration with others who don't share the same commitment (the white filling), and then you ended with another positive statement—your motivation and pursuit of excellence (the dark cookie on the bottom). If stated correctly, your strengths will overshadow whatever weakness was mentioned.

____

____

____

____

____

____

____

QUESTION 8: Your background has been in a different industry than ours. What skills do you feel you have that qualifies you for this position?

Everyone has skills that are transferable from one industry to another. Remember, you've been invited in to interview because the hiring manager needs your help and saw something in your resume shows you had the skills and experience they can use. Remember, the whole reason they reviewed your background was to find someone who could help solve his or her problems.

If you are leaving the military, you're obviously not being interviewed for your industry experience, so focus on those transferable skills that you have as they relate to the specific job at hand. Remember your leadership traits. Every service has a listing. For example, if you're in the infantry, you obviously realize that every company needs excellent managers with leadership capabilities, regardless of the product, service, or job being offered. Never say,

> *"I was just a grunt," or "I was just part of the infantry."*

If you have had limited civilian work since leaving the military, try to tie that experience into the military to make your work history longer and more applicable to the job for which you are being interviewed. For example:

> *"I took a position with a local retailer right after the military to make sure I had a smooth transition to civilian employment. I am now ready and*

confident that with my military training and experience I can be an asset for your company in this position."

____

____

____

____

____

____

____

____

____

QUESTION 9: Can you give me an example of your approach to problem solving?

Your answer to this question should demonstrate your critical thinking skills in solving problems in a logical way. Use a real-life example of a problem you solved in the past that was related to your work experience.

While the example you may give is unique to you, I would suggest your response could be something like this:

"Well, where I came from in the service, time was our enemy. We had to think very fast, assess any and all risks quickly, and then take effective action. If a mistake was made, someone could get hurt. So I'm really good at assessing an immediate issue and taking the necessary steps to resolve that issue. It wasn't that way all the time, however. If given a longer period of time, I first gather as much information as possible, including asking others for relevant input. This helps me gain a clear understanding of the problem. Then I begin to formulate possible solutions, again inviting input from others. Once I've evaluated each potential solution, I then select the one that, in my judgment, would be the most effective in solving the problem. Let me give you an example..."

QUESTION 10: Tell me about a time when you were unable to accomplish a key objective.

Your answer to this question, similar to most interview questions, requires you to give an example or tell a story. In this case, it's important to try and identify a situation that was beyond your control. Your position, company or industry could change at any time. Projects that you were working on could be redirected or killed altogether. Whatever your story, don't make it personal by volunteering any negative information about yourself that affected your ability to meet your goals. Be brief and specific.

QUESTION 11: What did/do your subordinates think of you?

Honesty is important when answering this question. You may not have been personal friends with each of your subordinates. Nevertheless, as a manager, you were able to maintain a positive working relationship.

The interviewer does **not** want to hear about any issues you had with officers or subordinates. This is a fishing question to see how you supervise and respond to a question like this.

Remembering that you are a manager now, your response may be:

> *"I'm confident that my subordinates have high regard for me as a manager. I'm sure that they would characterize me as someone who's ethical, has open communication, treats them fairly and has been able to develop a good working relationship based on mutual respect and trust."*

QUESTION 12: What have you learned from your experience in the service/military?

A hiring manager asking this question doesn't want to hear how you've learned to be on time for work, never leave early, or not to eat lunch at your desk. On the contrary, they want to hear one or two things that you've learned from your service experience that have increased your value as an employee. Focus on your skills that are relevant to the position you're targeting.

For example, if you're interviewing for a senior project manager position, your response may be:

> *"The service was my first real job. I came right out of high school (small little town, dead end job, etc.) and it instilled confidence in me. I learned how to handle multiple tasks at the same time and to be an effective manager. It was tough, but I am very proud of what I accomplished in my [insert number here] years in the (Army, Air Force, Marine Corps, Navy, Coast Guard, etc.)."*

You may then want to discuss any similarities you know between your military training, duties, and the job you are interviewing for.

Note: Make sure you know the details of the position(s) before you take an interview! Go online to places like LinkedIn and the company website to learn the keywords and tasks associated with the job and the company!

QUESTION 13: If I were to ask one or two of your former bosses, how would they view your performance?

This is a great opportunity to use your Management Endorsements. You'll find my discussion of this great marketing tool in the Packaging and Product Demonstration milestones of TheHireRoad™ as well as written examples.

Instead of the typical candidate response:

> *"Well, I'm sure they would say that I'm a hard worker, loyal and dedicated,"*

you'll be able to separate yourself from your competition with these written endorsements from former managers. Use this suggested response:

> *"I'm glad you asked that question because I'm very proud of what my former managers have said about my performance. Let me show you some examples."*

Now, get your old fitness reports, if you have them, and grab those one-liners that make you a star. If you don't have fitness reports you may have awards that you may be able to use. If neither, then you will have to contact your former bosses and ask for endorsements.

QUESTION 14: This company is constantly changing. How do you react to change? How flexible are you?

Remember that companies today are doing more with less. Every employee must be willing to be cross-trained and should focus on enhancing the value he represents to the employer. This means remaining flexible and open to change.

A suggested response to this question would be:

"With business and technology constantly changing, it's very important for me to be as flexible as possible in order to accommodate that change. It's easy for me to go with the flow and I enjoy working in a dynamic environment. In the service we were always faced with new challenges that require you to be nimble on your feet and smart with the decisions that followed. Change is the only thing that remains constant."

QUESTION 15: How do you measure success in general?

While everybody measures success in different ways, depending on personal situations, this question usually refers to your sense of security and well being. I suggest that in defining how you measure success, you include both a personal and professional perspective.

Your response may be:

> *"For me, success is measured by achieving a work-life balance and knowing that I'm doing the best I possibly can to provide for my family while at the same time achieving professional growth and helping my employer succeed."*

____

____

____

____

____

____

____

____

____

____

QUESTION 16: What did you enjoy the most about your last job/ experience in the service?

If you've already left the service, respond positively and explain that you enjoyed everything about your job. Focus on those responsibilities you had that reflect your strengths and try to relate them to the job you're currently interviewing for.

If you're still employed or currently still in the service, again you want to talk about the responsibilities you currently have that tie in with the job you're applying for. Talk about those enjoyable aspects of your work that bring out your strengths, such as project management or team leadership. Emphasize that this position you're now exploring gives you an even greater opportunity to demonstrate those strengths.

"In the service everyone was on board with what we had to do. Even if we had disagreements we got through them and got the job done on time and on target. Camaraderie was also great. My boss always said, 'One team, one fight, and one mission: Deliver the promise to succeed.'"

____

____

____

____

____

____

____

____

____

____

QUESTION 17: What did you enjoy the LEAST about your last job / experience in the service?

This is a tricky question, so let me suggest how **not** to respond. Don't give in to the temptation to say something bad about anyone or anything! **Do not** say something like:

"Well, I didn't like working fourteen hours a day," or "I was never given the resources necessary to do the job." or "My manager never fully explained what my responsibilities were day to day." ***This is a no-go situation!***

These responses are all negative in their tone, and they may reveal personal characteristics that could screen you out. The hiring manager may interpret from your responses that you're not fully committed to your work, you lack resourcefulness, or you find it difficult to work independently and make decisions on your own.

Your response needs to have a positive spin. You may want to mention a situation on your last job where you had to accept things as they were instead of what you would have liked them to be. Or, your response could acknowledge one aspect of your job that you disliked, such as routine paperwork. For example, you may say:

> *"There were very few things I disliked about the military as a whole. We had good communications and we took care of each other. The 13-month deployments were very tough on my family. Not being there when they needed me was tough, but that is over now. I don't mind traveling, but that was a bit extreme."*

Always end on a positive note.

____

____

____

____

____

____

____

____

____

____

QUESTION 18: What personal characteristics would you bring to this job?

Your response to this question allows you to point out personal traits that are valued by **any** company. They include: loyalty, enthusiasm, discipline, strong work ethic, dedication, professionalism, flexibility, the ability to work in a team environment, excellent interpersonal skills, respect for others, and a sense of humor.

A suggested response would be:

"In addition to my skills and abilities, I'm very proud of the ethical and professional approach I bring to my work. I also adapt to change very quickly. The military was an environment of constant change."

____

____

____

____

____

____

____

____

QUESTION 19: Do you prefer to work alone or work in a team environment?

Your response needs to stress the fact that you believe that teamwork is the most important contributor to a company's success. You prefer to work in a team environment. While your position, such as a copywriter or website developer, may require you to work alone, you're still part of a larger team all focused on a common goal. The important sentiment to convey here is that you have the ability to work well both independently and in a team environment.

Your response may be:

"I believe teamwork to be the most important component in a company's success. In fact, I believe that the ability to work with others is crucial to succeed not only in your career, but in your life. I've always enjoyed working in a team environment. After all, the military is ***one big team.*** *However I realize that sometimes it's necessary to work independently, which is* ***also*** *something taught in the military—you know, an Army of One. So it's easy for me to work in both environments and do whatever is necessary to be successful."*

___

___

___

___

___

___

___

___

___

___

QUESTION 20: Where do you see yourself in five years?

I'm not sure of the relevance of this question for hiring a new employee. However, it gets frequently asked in interviews! Hiring managers may like to get an idea of your career plans for the next several years but let's be realistic. Career planning has become career coping. As long as you're working for someone else, your five-year career plan can change in a heartbeat.

A good response to this question may be:

"Well, with business and technology changing so rapidly along with the uncertainty of the economy, it's really difficult for me to say exactly where I'll be in five years. I can tell you the type of company I'd like to be a part of: a company that's progressive, stable, and provides a challenging work environment where I can continue to grow professionally, make a significant contribution, and be compensated fairly for my efforts."

____

____

____

____

____

____

____

____

____

____

QUESTION 21: This position requires certain skills that aren't reflected/listed on your resume. Do you feel that you're still qualified for the position?

Keep in mind that every job description is basically a wish list. There's no such thing as a perfect candidate who happens to meet every specific skill the position requires. Companies select candidates to interview based on how closely they match the requirements of the position.

Ask the hiring manager to clarify what specific skills he's referring to. Odds are these skills will not be essential to the successful performance of the job. If they were, you wouldn't have been invited in to interview.

Your response could be:

"While I may not have the specific skills you mentioned, I do believe I'm well qualified for this position. I am fast learner and would certainly be willing to learn whatever's necessary to excel in this position. I also adapt to change very quickly. The military was an environment of constant change."

____

____

____

____

____

____

____

____

____

____

QUESTION 22: What did you learn in the service and/or school that you feel could apply to this job?

Regardless of how little you have completed in the way of your formal education in your career so far, your response to this question must include some characteristics that highlight the positive approach you take to your work.

Your response could be;

"I think one of the most important things I learned while I was in school, and in the service, was self-discipline. This includes how to meet deadlines, how to apply myself in terms of establishing goals and achieving them, and the development of good analytical and problem-solving skills. I also learned how to multitask, as I had to handle several classes while working part time.

I have read many case studies where teamwork was a critical theme for the successful completion of projects. The military was all about teamwork and completing the mission. We learned from the mistakes of others, saving us time and lives for sure."

____

____

____

____

____

____

____

____

____

____

And finally, the **big two questions** almost always asked in an interview:

QUESTION 23: Why should we hire you?

This question gives you the opportunity to discuss your skills, experience, expertise, and style as they relate to the company and the job you're interviewing for. This is where you get to make a solid sales pitch on how your military skills and education/training can help the company meet its needs. You should have done research on the company and the position before the interview so try to be as specific as you can, such as:

"My experience with supply and warehousing is a perfect fit for this logistics position," or "My supervisory and training skills in computer security in my last posting is a perfect fit for your IT security needs at XYZ company," or "My training in emergency response is a great fit for your OSHA compliance officer needs."

If you don't have a good specific match between your previous experience or training, remember that your value is measured in terms of time and money, so as you discuss your potential contributions to the position and the company, be sure to relate them to profitability. Employment is all about solving problems, and solving problems increases profitability. The bottom line **is** the bottom line.

Your response may be:

"Obviously you feel I have the skills and experience necessary to help you solve your problems and increase profitability. Otherwise, you wouldn't have invited me here today. However, in addition to making an immediate contribution to your bottom line, I would also bring to your organization maturity, experience, and an ethical and professional approach to my work."

If you're interviewing for a position where a security clearance is required, you may want to include:

"Also, with a current secret DoD clearance, you'll save the time and money associated with a thorough background check. My last background investigation was completed [insert date here]."

QUESTION 24: What salary are you looking for?

This question is often asked at the conclusion of the interview and seems to be the hardest one to answer! This one is especially tricky if you are feeling desperate for a job.

Regardless of when this question is asked during the interview process, don't name a specific number. If really pressed, give only a range. **Before the interview** you should have an idea of the range for the position based on your research into the job, company, and industry. Ask around. Use websites like LinkedIn and others where you can get estimates.

If this question is asked at the beginning of the interview, your response should be something like:

> *"At this point in our discussion, I don't have enough information about the requirements of the position and how my skills and abilities can meet your specific needs. I'm sure toward the end of our meeting I'll be in a better position to discuss compensation."*

If this question is asked at the end of the interview, your response should be something like,

> *"Well, based on our discussion today, I think this position is a great fit for me professionally and for your company/organization. I'm sure whatever offer you'd make to me would be very fair."*
>
> OR . . .
>
> *"I have done some research on your industry and comparable positions so I know the range you normally offer and would be comfortable with whatever you think is appropriate. You know your needs and what is fair and appropriate for someone with my skills."*

Try **not** to give a number. That is for the employer to provide. If you have done your research before the interview you should be aware of what dollar value is fair for the position and what is an insult. Let the employer explain the salary and benefits to you—let them sell you on taking the offer.

____

____

____

____

____

To succeed in your job search in our new economy requires creativity, a willingness to think outside the box, and innovative approaches to effectively meet the challenges of finding employment. Things have changed. Times have changed and times are tough. This means new tools, a completely new approach, and a new line of attack.

Preparation is the key to job hunting success—especially in the interview! TheHireRoad™ Job Search system includes a unique audio interview CD. The CD has questions that are designed to let you rehearse your answers whenever and wherever you can listen to the audio. Imagine being able to review potential questions and suggested answers before each interview. This can make the interview process for military veterans as easy as 1-2-3:

1. Practice with 69 different questions you may be asked by the hiring manager as well as by human resources.
2. Then listen to the 15 questions that **you** should potentially ask the hiring manager!
3. Add these special military veteran questions to your arsenal and you should be prepared for whatever they may ask!

SECTION 4

Pay Day!

INTRODUCTION

Negotiating Your True Worth, Not a Salary

One of the most difficult things for job seekers is determining a fair offer for employment. We in the military know what everyone makes. No cloak and dagger stuff; it's public knowledge. The funny part is you always wondered why the hell a second lieutenant gets paid so much. Answer: They're a college graduate. But I digress. Milestone Four is where you'll negotiate the difference between what you're offered and your true worth to the organization. Transitioning military personnel have to be very careful to understand the range of income. There is a difference between what you need to survive and what you deserve or want. Military veterans, who lack knowledge and experience in how salaries are set, and what bonuses should be offered, can be taken advantage of. That's what we'll discuss in this section.

So welcome to the final section in TheHireTactics™ series and **MILESTONE 4: Pricing.** In the next chapters you will learn more about the process and how to ensure you are receiving a compensation package that is worthy of your skills and experience!

CHAPTER TEN

They Made You a Job Offer!

YOU GOT AN OFFER!

Well-deserved congratulations! All of your efforts have paid off. You've completed the interview process, become the preferred solution, and now the company wants to enter into a relationship with you. You will have received either a written or verbal job offer and the delicate dance between you as the job seeker and your potential employer over what you will be paid really begins.

Many job search systems and guidebooks leave this chapter out because talking about money after all the time and effort it took to get your job seems anti-climatic. After all, you wanted a job and now you have one. You should be able to trust the employer to make a fair offer right?

Wrong!

This is the most critical step in establishing your true worth to the company. How you position yourself now at the beginning of your relationship will continue throughout your career with this company! You want to receive a package that is fair, reasonable, and reflects your worth to the company. Your employer on the other hand, wants to get you for as low a cost as they reasonably can without insulting you.

The offer will usually contain a title or level, an outline of your total compensation package, starting date, and location. But there may be a big difference between what they're offering and what you're worth. It is your job to ensure your price and their offer reflects your true worth to the organization.

Obviously, if the offer meets or exceeds your expectations, you should consider accepting it as presented. However, if the offer falls short of meeting your expectations, you need to negotiate.

If you've been out of work for some time you're obviously going to be feeling a great sense of relief. It can be very tempting to accept the offer as is and start the job right away. But keep in mind, there's a strong possibility that you can negotiate a better compensation package, depending on your leverage.

I know that negotiating a salary is totally foreign to military personnel. Your salary comes from a table someone in the Pentagon created with who knows what input. Your rank and years in service pretty much determine what your salary and benefits will be. Nothing to negotiate or anyone to negotiate with!

As you carefully assess the various components of your job offer, understand that almost every one of these components can be negotiated! Few companies extend offers that are accepted at face value, and negotiation is expected. Not negotiating can actually be a negative sign to a new employer.

The information that follows will help you understand how to assess your needs and requirements, determine your worth, evaluate the offer, and then negotiate for more.

ACKNOWLEDGING YOUR OFFER

It is customary for the hiring manager to verbally extend an offer to you. Sometimes it will happen at the close of the interview (or the final interview if you‘ve done more than one). Sometimes it will be a telephone call a few days after the interview. Depending on the position, the offer may come from the hiring manager, your new manager-to-be, or from human resources.

If you get a verbal offer make sure you understand the job title, job responsibilities, salary, start date, and benefits. Then ask for the offer in writing.

It is not a job offer until it is in writing. Kinda' like "it ain't pay day until the check cashes."

After you've received the written offer, contact the hiring manager immediately and express your thanks for the written offer. Then ask for at least one or two days to evaluate it before giving your acceptance. Make sure you ask if there is a deadline for your decision. Some offers will include expiration dates, especially if there is a pressing need or project deadline associated with the position.

You can send a formal acceptance letter or a simple thank-you, depending on the offer and your planned response. If you want time to negotiate, the thank-you note and a request for a few days to review and consider the offer is perfect—classy and professional.

If you're entertaining offers from several different companies, you may want to ask for even more time. However, never take longer than the hiring manager is willing to provide. There is a thin line between a reasonable time to consider an offer and appearing indecisive.

It's gratifying to know that at this point in the entire process **you** now have the tactical advantage! You have the high ground and the most **power**. The company has decided they want **you**. They have invested their time and energy in selecting you, so based on this leverage, take advantage and negotiate the best possible package.

JOB TYPES

In today's economy there are several job categories including temporary, holiday, contract, and part-time being offered to job seekers. But our focus is job offers for full-time positions.

Note that there are two types of full-time employees—hourly and salaried. Hourly is usually a lower income, less responsible position. You are literally paid for the hours you work and have to punch in and punch out on a clock or computer. There are usually strict state or local rules on overtime, breaks, and benefits. Hourly wages are set by the state as minimum wage or by a contract through a union or other group. Benefits and perks are limited. This means there is generally little to no flexibility on the part of the employer.

The other paid position is called salaried. Salaried employees are not on the clock and while you may have regular hours from 8 a.m. to 5 p.m., you are expected to work as long as a job takes. There may be regular breaks and/or lunch hours but if you work through them or work an occasional 60-hour week, there is no additional salary. Management or other professional jobs are usually salaried positions.

Both types of full-time positions can benefit from using TheHireTactics™ milestones in Packaging, Promotion, and Product Demonstration. However, pricing is usually not applicable to hourly employees. So the balance of this book will focus on salaried employees where employers can be more flexible and negotiations are more likely.

OFFER COMPONENTS

Generally speaking your job offer will outline the salary, location, job title, and responsibilities. It may be specific on benefits or use a throw-away line like "standard employee benefits." If appropriate, there may be incentives or special bonuses.

Make sure you understand **exactly** what components are included in traditional offers for the position and the location. If you don't know, ask people in similar jobs. Use your network or ask in forums like LinkedIn. Knowledge is power and in this case, money in your pocket.

Most jobs (and your sense of value) are determined by your salary. Well before you have your first interview, do your salary research! Gather outside information on the current market value of your position. Credible Internet resources for this information include Salary.com, Payscale.com, Jobstar.org, and Indeed.com. Their tools should give you a good market rate for the salary of peers in your position in your local area. Salary is obviously the most important piece of your job offer but it is **not** the only part!

Don't overlook important items such as bonuses, commissions, expenses for moving, etc., that put cash in your pocket. But don't be distracted by visions of huge commission or bonus checks. Always start with the **known** base salary.

Keep in mind that key components found in most job offers vary from one company to the next. Depending on the job and the industry there may be other components such as a uniform allowance or child care. These other components could have a major impact on your decision to accept or reject the offer. Take health coverage for example, where the scope of coverage will vary extensively between employers. While that may not be important to a healthy 20-something college graduate, it may be critical to a family with children. *Note:* If you are retired military you may want to address additional compensation since you already have full medical benefits and the company does not have to pay for that part of your hiring package!

You should also be aware of the specific job responsibilities, the reporting structure, vacation time, how you'll be paid, your start date, and your hours. Evaluate these components carefully to make sure they fall in line with your requirements.

It's essential that you understand all the benefits you'll receive, as well as company policies and procedures. If not included with your written offer, call the HR department and ask for a written explanation of benefits and an employee handbook. The larger the company, the more likely it is that benefits will be standardized for employees at various levels.

It is imperative that you create a checklist and evaluate every component of your offer. As you create your checklist you'll see there are quite a number of items that you can negotiate as part of your overall total compensation package. It's important that you review this list carefully, identifying those components that you want included in your offer. When considering your offer letter you really need to think about your value to the employer.

YOUR WORTH IN THE MARKETPLACE

Worth versus price is an ongoing discussion for job seekers. You are only worth what the other person thinks you are worth! That means worth is in the eye of the beholder or in this case, your employer! Sadly, your value or worth to an employer may be quite different from what you actually perceive your worth to be. This fact is especially hard for experienced employees entering new positions or new industries.

The value or worth of an employee is largely based on supply and demand. If you are in the pool with a lot of job applicants with similar skills and experience, you may have become a commodity. Being a commodity means you look like everyone else and are replaceable with just about any other candidate. Commodities are generally purchased cheaply.

However, most companies are usually willing to pay market price for a position if the job seeker is worth the investment. So it becomes critical you know what that market price is and how to position and sell yourself for the highest possible value. How do you find out your worth in the marketplace?

Basically, you have to research competitive salary ranges and benefits for similar positions in the same industry in the same geography while keeping in mind the supply and demand for your particular skills. If accepting the offer means relocating to another area, don't forget to take into consideration the cost-of-living differential since this will most certainly impact your walk-away point. There are a number of resources online to help you determine your worth in the marketplace, including:

www.Payscale.com
www.JobSearchIntelligence.com
www.SalaryCalculator.com
www.Salary.com
http://calculator.GIJobs.com
http://militarypay.defense.gov/pay/calc/index.htm

I would also go to www.BankRate.com to get a good comparison for cost of living differentials based on geographic location. Also visit your transition office or Family Service Center to attain the latest website information.

Typically, there's a big difference between what a company is willing to pay you, what you can reasonably expect, and what you'd like to be paid. There is nothing sinister or evil in this reality. Whenever we plan on making a purchase, such as a new car, refrigerator, TV, or stereo, we always want to get the best product at the lowest price. We want to get the best deal.

A company is no exception. Employers want to invest as little as they can to solve their problems. That means buying equipment and hiring employees for as little as they can, yet retaining the best value and talent. Corporations with stockholders actually have a legal fiduciary responsibility to try to acquire your services at the lowest possible investment!

While you may perceive yourself as a legend in your own mind, and therefore the greatest thing since sliced bread, the package you're offered may be lower than what you're expecting. This happens because the company would obviously like to acquire your talent at the lowest price. Your best defense is to do the research necessary to know your true worth.

For example, the company may have internally established a salary range of $65,000 to $85,000 a year with a moving bonus if asked. But they've made you an offer of $70,000 a year and no bonuses which they use as an opening offer. However, your research shows you should reasonably expect at least $80,000 based on your experience and expect a relocation bonus. Sharing your research will help you negotiate a better offer. This is why knowing the position's worth in the marketplace ahead of time is so critical.

SPECIAL NOTE FOR NEWLY TRANSITIONED VETERANS

If you have recently separated from the military, your target company may consider you a hiring risk.

Why? Because you are an unknown entity.

Though you have management and leadership experience, you are viewed as having no experience in Corporate America. Hopefully you took care of that by properly packaging yourself in the very first contact with this employer (see **SECTION 1** *Veteran Employment Tactics* in this book for more information on how to position yourself).

Play it smart! Look, listen, and learn, just like you did in the military. Once you establish yourself in the "new world" you have proved yourself as an employee who adds value and will be in a better position to negotiate future prospects.

Loyalty seldom exists in your new world like it did in the military. There is a saying, "Loyalty is paycheck to paycheck." Sad, but so very true. I did not believe it when I first heard it, but it is sometimes more true than the civilian world admits.

CHAPTER ELEVEN

Key Considerations

BE PREPARED

To be successful in negotiation you must thoroughly prepare for that negotiation. This begins by determining your key considerations. These are the components that you've identified ahead of time as must-haves in a job offer. Once these are identified, the next step is to compare your key considerations to the major components of your offer. This will help you identify those issues to be negotiated.

I can't emphasize this enough: Your ability to successfully negotiate key considerations requires research and background information. Having that knowledge can mean the difference between accepting and rejecting an offer. And you do not want to accept or reject an offer based on assumptions and lack of data!

Your key considerations are your must-haves. These are things you consider as critical in any offer and are unique to you. However, most include items such as base salary, incentive programs, health insurance, retirement plan, minimum vacation, relocation expenses, company car or car allowance, etc. You need to make a list based on your research and expectations.

It's also important that you understand all the additional benefits you'll receive, as well as company policies and procedures. If these are not included with your written offer, call the HR department and ask for a written explanation of benefits and an employee handbook.

CASH COMPENSATION

Now let's focus on what is usually the most important key consideration: cash compensation. It's almost always at the top of the must-have list, and rightly so. While the total package may contain other attractive components, your offer obviously has to be financially viable for you to even consider it. Being in the military you may find this to be a challenge. Whether you have been in for four years or more than 20 years, determining your value-add and equating it to a dollar value can be challenging and will require some thinking. Remember, thousands of veterans are out there to help so don't forget to ask for guidance.

Cash compensation typically includes a base salary and some form of incentive pay, such as bonuses or commission. Only the base salary should be defined as a key consideration, since this represents the fixed amount of income you'll be receiving, as compared to a bonus or commission which is variable. Start with this number because everything else will likely be outside your employer's control. For example, you cannot count on commissions or bonuses because you do not control the client's sales decision. And remember, a bonus is not a guarantee. Many companies discontinue or just provide the minimum bonuses during rough times. In addition, the IRS takes about 30 percent of that bonus prior to the physical payout. I'd rather have a bigger paycheck than a possible bonus.

You need to determine the absolute minimum base salary required to meet your everyday obligations. If you haven't already determined what this number should be, your first homework assignment will be to carefully assess your financial needs to arrive at what I call your **walk-away number.**

While you were in the military, compensation like BAQ, BAH, VHA, and/or BAS were not taxable income. All of your paycheck is now taxable. Beware of the military calculators many sites provide. They are a great guide, but I have found them to be off by 10 to 20 percent for true walk-away numbers.

How do you determine your walk-away number? Look at all your monthly bills and figure out what amount is needed to meet those obligations. Remember to use after-tax figures and don't forget to factor in your spouse's fixed income, if any.

Note: Some states do not tax military pay while on active duty. I lived in California most of my active duty time and was not required to pay California income tax because my residence was listed as Florida. Of course, California now takes its fair share for sure. Also, some states like Nevada, Texas, and others do not tax your military retirement income, which is a huge benefit. If you've been declared disabled, you may even have a property tax waiver as well. Use the sample *Financial Analysis Worksheet* in the Summary and Conclusion to help you assess your walk-away number.

This exercise will provide you with a number that represents the absolute minimum you need to earn as a base salary. This then becomes your walk-away number. Even though there may be variables which surface during negotiation that may impact your walk-away number, knowing this number ahead of time will help you determine if the final offer is financially viable.

Unfortunately, many people in transition fail to go through this exercise, and because they've been out of work for some time, they become desperate and accept a position where the salary is insufficient to meet their needs. They discover this several weeks into their new job, become financially stressed, and begin to think about looking for a higher-paying job. This is **not** what you want to do.

What if a job offer has been made and, even after negotiation, the most the employer will offer is still less than your bottom-line (no-go) number? What should you do to ensure you are making the right decision?

Stick to your base salary number!

The whole reason to know your walk-away number is to help you make the right decision. You won't have to stress over accepting the offer. If you don't hit your salary goal, you agree to part ways. You say, "I'm really sorry we weren't able to make it work, but I'm going to have to pass."

Did that scare you?

What if you have been out of work for months and this is the first sure-thing you've gotten? Shouldn't you take it and work really, really hard to get a raise?

This is a recipe for disaster. You will be starting a new job knowing you settled for less than you are worth. You will likely become resentful and an unhappy employee. Also, the employer has now established that you can be bought cheaply. They are not likely to respect you or worry about you leaving in the future.

BEWARE IF YOU ARE RETIRED MILITARY!

It will be very apparent to employers in your biography and your post-interview packet that you are retired military. Because of this your military retirement pay may become a topic during salary negotiations. You explain to your employer that your retirement pay is no different than a civilian retirement savings account much like a 401K, an IRA, or an annuity. You should tell them that most military members did not have the 401K benefit or other saving plans while they were in the military and the retirement income makes up for that.

If the subject comes up, address without hesitation and call it your 401K, not a retirement. Educate your possible future employer that in the military we did not have the same salary structure, bonus plans, and stock options as the current market you are entering. As a replacement, the Federal Government provides a monthly annuity. Be polite.

In truth, your military retirement income and its amount is really none of anyone's business and should not become part of the negotiation of your salary. But it may come up and you should be prepared to address it. Still, remember you are having a conversation, not an interview.

Remember to stick to your base salary and calculate your base salary without taking into account your military retirement compensation!

If your possible future employer wants to include your retirement income in negotiations then maybe they are not the right employer or company for you. A good employer will not pay you less because you have additional income.

Think of it this way. If you have a spouse, should they pay you less because your spouse contributes to the total family compensation in the family? Or take it even further—if you have a roommate should they pay you less because you are not paying the full rent amount? Of course not.

Companies that use this practice usually lose their employees after a few years or even less. They may be taking advantage of your lack of expertise in the area of career management and negotiations. Just play it smart.

MUST-HAVES

Once you've established your walk-away number, your next homework assignment is to identify any remaining key considerations, or **must-haves.** Remember, these will influence your decision to accept or reject the offer. Don't skip this step or take it lightly. I have seen job seekers take jobs based on the salary only to become disenchanted and even lose money because they neglected these other items!

Typical must-haves may include:

- Work schedule (days, evenings, shift work, extensive overtime without compensation)
- Commute time
- Business travel
- Health care benefits and percentage share
- Vacation
- Education benefits
- Retirement plans (401K, stock plan, pension, etc.)

- Moving bonus or housing allowance (important if you are moving from a low-cost area in the Midwest to an area with a high-cost of living, like Los Angeles or New York City)
- Working environment (indoors, outdoors, high risk)
- Lifestyle friendliness (domestic partner benefits, etc.)
- Tenure, work guarantees
- Advancement potential
- Military friendly
- Involvement in the veteran community
- Others which may be unique to you

You might find that, although the majority of your requirements are met, there may be certain aspects that make the offer unacceptable. These could include the **red flags** you identified during the interview process, such as extensive travel or a potential merger which may adversely affect your position. Just like the walk-away salary number, determine if there are any walk-away must-haves.

Make the list as complete as you can. This will help ensure you don't regret it later.

COMPANY LIFE CYCLE

Once you've identified your own personal key considerations and established your walk-away number, look at the company's life cycle.

All companies go through several stages in their lifespan. They begin as start-ups, enter growth periods, and if lucky, become stable. As we've seen in the current economy, they can also be struggling or in decline. Where they are and how long they expect to be there will directly impact many of the major components of your job offer. Therefore, knowing this will help you understand your worth in the marketplace, interpret their offer more rationally, and allow you to negotiate more effectively.

If you're considering joining a start-up company, you can expect the salary to be low, the incentives like stock ownership to be high, the benefits to be low to none, and the perks to be low. You should also expect there will be no stability or long-term employment potential until the company has survived at least five years.

On the other hand, if the company is in a growth mode, the salary, incentives, benefits, and perks will usually be competitive. If the company is well established, you can typically expect a higher salary, low incentives and benefits, and higher perks, as well as the potential for longer-term employment.

Google the company. Check out employer review websites such as Glassdoor.com to see if there are rumors of takeovers or imminent bankruptcy. Are they publicly traded or privately held? If you want to be promoted and there are family members in the organization, there could easily be family politics. These are all red flags.

CHAPTER TWELVE

The Art of Negotiation

BASIS FOR NEGOTIATION

Your leverage in the negotiation process will depend on how much your skills are needed by the company.

If the skills you bring to the table are in short supply, your leverage may be considerable. On the other hand if your skills are in plentiful supply (e.g., you are a commodity), you may have very little leverage, so be careful.

As outlined in the prior chapters, you need to do the research necessary to know your worth in the marketplace and the price the potential employer should pay for the location and tasks. This is the starting point as you begin negotiations.

This is strategic and tactical information you **must have** in order to win the salary and worth battle. You do not want to be combative but you must stand up for your value and the value you bring as a veteran!

THE PROCESS OF NEGOTIATION

In simple terms, negotiation is the resolution of differences through discussion and collaboration. It involves working together to explore each other's expectations with the objective of finding mutually acceptable ways to satisfy them. The key word here is mutually acceptable. You want the proverbial win-win scenario where each party feels good about some part of the eventual deal.

Negotiation is **not** an exercise where there's one winner and one loser. While it's natural to feel some anxiety, enter into the process of negotiation with a positive attitude. Use your power of influence to reach the goal of establishing a win-win situation.

Remember though, you'll most likely be negotiating with your future boss. This will hopefully be a long-term relationship, so try to avoid any situation that may negatively affect it. Be professional and firm but not rude or demanding.

BUYING SIGNALS

Initial negotiation may have begun during the interview when you started receiving buying signals from the hiring manager. Such signals indicate that you're seriously being considered as the preferred solution. For example, the hiring manager may have begun selling you on the benefits of working for the company, initiated a discussion about compensation, or the conversation became more about problem-solving as if you were already employed by the company. Another signal is the interview may have run much longer than scheduled or the hiring manager introduced you to others with whom you were not originally scheduled to meet. These are all positive buying signals.

If the hiring manager **has** decided that you're the best fit for the position, he or she may initiate a discussion concerning certain terms of your compensation package on the spot. When this occurs, regardless of what you negotiate and agree to during the interview process, **always** make sure it's reflected in your written offer.

PROS AND CONS OF YOUR OFFER

Having received the written offer, you need to look carefully at all the **pros** and **cons** associated with this position. Use the *Sample Job Offer Component Checklist* in the Summary and Conclusion of this book to help you prepare for effective negotiation and enable you to objectively determine whether or not to accept the final offer.

The *Job Offer Component Checklist* is by no means complete or customized to your unique situation and needs. There may be many other pros and cons associated with you and your family's position that need to be considered. So be sure to list as many positive and negative aspects of this position as you can.

DEAL BREAKERS

When making your pro-and-con list, be sure to include any conditions or potential job attributes that would make it impossible for you to say "yes" to the job. These are known as deal breakers. And again, these are unique to you and your family situation. One applicant's deal breaker may be another applicant's throw-away item.

Deal breakers are just that, facets of the job that simply cannot be negotiated away. For example, if you are a single parent with young children, a position with extensive overnight travel or long commutes would not only be a con, it could be a potential deal breaker.

LEGITIMATE ISSUES TO NEGOTIATE

After you've identified your pros and cons, look at the list of cons and identify those that are legitimate and reasonable to negotiate. Salary and benefits are usually legitimate issues to negotiate. Another may be excessive travel as would the necessity to work long hours which are common in start-up companies.

Check to see which items are flexible with your potential employer and which are iron-clad and in concrete. Asking if they may be flexible is the first step in negotiation and depending on the answer may turn a con into a deal breaker.

THROW-AWAY ITEMS

Now look again at the cons and see which could be throw-away items in the negotiation. These are the items you'd like to negotiate more in your favor. However, your inability to do so will not affect your decision to accept the offer. You put them on the table to see if you can improve them but would not walk away if they remain as originally offered.

A good example of a throw-away item would be vacation. Let's say you've been accustomed to four weeks vacation per year and your potential employer is offering two. You may ask for three, or even four, but if you don't get the additional weeks it won't affect your decision to accept the offer.

Another example is a sign-on bonus. In today's economy these are rare and often considered a throw-away item unless it happens to be a standard in the industry or you happen to have an exceptional or rare skill.

STRATEGIES TO NEGOTIATE A HIGHER BASE SALARY

There's no need to approach the subject of base salary if you've negotiated an acceptable number during the interview process, or if the offer includes a number above what you expected. However, if you need to negotiate, there are several strategies that may get you a higher base salary:

STRATEGY #1

Make sure the salary you're offered is reflective of the industry standards that you researched prior to the interview. If not, let the hiring manager know that you've done your research and the offer falls short of what is reasonable.

When negotiating salary, the old saying applies: "Whoever names a number first loses." Therefore, let the hiring manager name a specific number first. If that number is not in line with industry standards and there's no adjustment made, you may need to rethink your intention of accepting the offer. Remember, companies should pay market value for your skills.

Assuming the salary is within the acceptable range for the industry, but lower than expected, your first strategy is to ask the manager if there's any wiggle room to that base salary number. This is a warm and fuzzy way of saying you'd like to see the amount raised.

Don't suggest a specific dollar amount of increase, but rather let the hiring manager come back to you with a revised number. If you're comfortable with this number, express your agreement and move on to the next issue to be negotiated. If not, try the second strategy.

STRATEGY #2

Try to negotiate a salary increase based on short-term job performance. The majority of companies grant salary increases based on the outcome of yearly performance reviews. The strategy here is to negotiate a six-month, or even three-month review rather than waiting for the end of your first full year of employment. Ask for the opportunity to demonstrate just how well you can perform in your new job with the understanding that you'll both sit down in three or six months and review that performance. This can be a win-win situation because it puts the onus on you to deliver, and the manager is only agreeing to a review, not necessarily guaranteeing you a raise. A favorable review, however, will more than likely result in a bump in your base salary.

If there's no wiggle room, and the hiring manager has been reluctant to give you an early review, it's time to move on to the third strategy.

STRATEGY #3

Ask for a reconfiguration of your job responsibilities. In other words, ask for more responsibilities to be added to the position to justify a higher salary. This increases your value and should warrant a salary that meets your acceptable number. Very few candidates ask for additional responsibilities when negotiating an offer.

Despite your efforts at skillful negotiation, you may find that the hiring manager is unwilling or unable to increase the amount of base salary. He or she is also unwilling or unable to grant a short-term performance review, and there is no way the job responsibilities can be reconfigured. If this is the case there is one last strategy to try.

STRATEGY #4

Regardless of outcome, you may want to try and negotiate one of your throw-away items, such as a signing bonus or modified commission plan, as a means of increasing your first-year total compensation. A sign-on bonus is a one-time expense for the company and is not recurring. Again, don't name a number first when suggesting a sign-on bonus. Let the hiring manager come back to you with a number.

THE NEGOTIATION DISCUSSION

If you've been working with a search firm, let the recruiter do the negotiating. Make sure he or she understands ahead of time what your key considerations, requirements, and concerns are so the recruiter can effectively negotiate on your behalf. Be sure to let them know about any deal breakers!

There are many military recruiting firms and they make their money on volume of placements. If you are new to the job search battlefield, beware of them pushing you into a job or situation that leads to a poor placement. Hold firm and be patient. If you have followed TheHireTactics™, completed your research, done your homework, and know your value, you are in a good position to know what is fair for you. Don't let someone talk you into something beneath your dignity and experience.

If no search firm is involved, call the hiring manager directly and ask for a meeting to discuss certain terms of the offer. The ideal situation is to meet face-to-face; however, if that's not possible you can negotiate over the phone.

Avoid negotiating with human resources! They will be the enforcers of policy and history. It is also highly unlikely that they will be able to assess your worth in the position. They will have little to no decision-making authority. Generally speaking only the hiring manager can do that. Be respectful, but remember HR sometimes stands for "hiring resistance."

Begin your discussion by mentioning the **areas of agreement** in the offer. Easy ones will likely be location and job activities. Then transition into the specific items of concern to you, such as salary and benefits. Here's where your list of deal killers and throw-away items comes into play.

SUMMARY AND CONCLUSION

Once you receive the final, revised offer, take a step back and take one last look at your list of **pros** and **cons**. Then decide if this is truly the right opportunity for you.

Successful negotiation occurs when both parties are able to understand and resolve their respective differences in a reasonable way. Your attitude and demeanor will go a long way in achieving that goal. Always begin negotiation by expressing your desire to reach an equitable agreement.

Remember, even during negotiation you need to continue to **focus on the value** you bring to the organization. Emphasize how your performance will **impact profitability.** This is the **only** reason they want to hire you.

You've negotiated your compensation package, received the revised offer in writing, reviewed your final list of pros and cons, and now you're ready to begin your new job. The last step is to **confirm your acceptance, both verbally and in a letter to the hiring manager.**

And with that **congratulations**, you are now well on your way to being one of the lucky employed!

Welcome to "The HIRED Road!" You should now know what you are worth for the jobs you have sought and understand how to evaluate and negotiate to receive a fair price from your employer.

I hope we have freed you from the C.R.A.P. and have shown you how to avoid becoming a commodity in the job market and how to successfully use the interview to demonstrate your value. With the information in this section you should be able to negotiate the offer you both need and want.

I hope you have learned valuable skills that will ensure your successful transition now and when you need it in the future.

However, if you feel you need additional help and coaching in any of the four milestones, I humbly suggest you investigate the proven job search system TheHireRoad™ developed by my friend and coauthor Greg Wood, CCMP by visiting the website www.TheHireChallenge.com

Also, please feel free to contact me at TheHireTactics™ website with questions and suggestions for future books and articles.

FINANCIAL ANALYSIS WORKSHEET

You've had the interview! You've been offered a position! Now you must decide whether the salary offered meets your financial needs. This worksheet will help you efficiently compare your monthly expenses with your projected monthly net income. If your net income is higher than your monthly expenses, you can feel comfortable with the salary offered. However, if your expenses are higher than your income, it may be time to negotiate your salary.

MONTHLY ONGOING EXPENSES

Itemize costs that are ongoing each month ________________

Mortgage (including monthly property taxes) ________________

Rent (in lieu of mortgage OR in new location) ________________

Association fees(s) ________________

Utilities (gas, electric, water) ________________

Telephone ________________

Cable/Internet ________________

Car payments ________________

Insurance: ________________

- Health ________________
- Car ________________
- Homeowner ________________
- Life ________________

Child care/nanny ________________

Housekeeper/gardner ________________

Other unique to you ________________

ADD EVERYTHING TOGETHER FOR TOTAL MONTHLY ONGOING EXPENSES

TOTAL____ **(A)**

MONTHLY VARIABLE EXPENSES

This list is for those items you spend money on occasionally. These are things you could cut down, if necessary. Do this **twice**—once for your current expenses and once for your anticipated or revised budget with your new job. You are looking for opportunities to change your lifestyle to take a job that may have a low salary.

Current Budget

Clothing __________
  Dry cleaning __________
  Tailoring __________
Food __________
  Groceries __________
  Dining out __________
  Fast food __________
Transportation costs __________
  Gas __________
  Repairs (including oil changes) __________
  Car wash/wax __________
  Parking costs __________
  Public transportation __________
Leisure activities __________
  Vacations/trips __________
  Movies/Plays/Concerts __________
  Subscriptions __________
  Golf/Games __________
Gifts __________
Education __________
  College tuition __________
  Extension classes __________
  Books/supplies __________
Charitable contributions __________
Other __________

TOTAL ____________________ **(B)**

Revised Budget

Clothing	__________
Purchases	__________
Dry cleaning	__________
Tailoring	__________
Food	__________
Groceries	__________
Dining out	__________
Fast food	__________
Transportation costs	__________
Gas	__________
Repairs (incuding oil changes)	__________
Car wash/wax	__________
Parking costs	__________
Public transportation	__________
Leisure activities	__________
Vacations/trips	__________
Movies/plays/concerts	__________
Subscriptions	__________
Golf/games	__________
Gifts	__________
Education	__________
College tuition	__________
Extension classes	__________
Books/supplies	__________
Charitable contributions	__________
Other	__________

TOTAL ____________________ (C)

MONTHLY ESTIMATED NET INCOME

List all your sources of established and consistent monthly income (after taxes)

Proposed salary/wages	_______________
Commissions (average)	_______________
Bonuses (average)	_______________
Unemployment insurance	_______________
Severance pay	_______________
Alimony/child support	_______________
Investment interest	_______________
Rental property	_______________
Home-based business	_______________
Spouse salary	_______________
Other	_______________

TOTAL MONTHLY NET INCOME _______________________ (D)

MONTHLY BUDGET SUMMARY

Subtracting your total Monthly Ongoing Expenses and Monthly Variable Expenses from your Total Estimated Monthly Net Income will help you determine if you need to negotiate the salary offered for your new position.

TOTAL MONTHLY NET INCOME (D)	_______________
	Minus (-)
TOTAL MONTHLY ONGOING EXPENSES (A)	_______________
	Minus (-)
TOTAL MONTHLY VARIABLE EXPENSES (B) or (C)	_______________
	Equals (=)
NET MONTHLY DIFFERENCE	_______________

After subtracting your monthly expenses from your net income, if the net monthly difference has money to spare, the offer is probably acceptable. However, if the amount of spare money is in the negative, or the positive amount is not enough for you, you may want to renegotiate the proposed salary.

JOB OFFER COMPONENT CHECKLIST

Sample Pros (pluses for you)

- Stable company ☐
- Growth industry ☐
- Global market share ☐
- Like potential boss ☐
- Like potential coworkers ☐
- Good reputation ☐
- Prospect for advancement ☐
- Occasional overseas travel ☐
- Sign-on bonus ☐
- Expense account ☐
- Excellent benefits ☐
- Corner office/two windows ☐
- Military friendly ☐
- Military experience in top management ☐
- Active in veteran's causes ☐
- Patriotic ☐
- Same political persuasion as me ☐

Your personal pros from the job:

- ______________________________ ☐
- ______________________________ ☐
- ______________________________ ☐
- ______________________________ ☐
- ______________________________ ☐
- ______________________________ ☐
- ______________________________ ☐
- ______________________________ ☐

Sample Cons (negatives for you)

- Base salary too low ☐
- Possible future relocation(s) ☐
- No company car ☐
- Low monthly car allowance ☐
- Lengthy commute each way ☐
- 60–70% road travel on the job ☐
- Only one week vacation first year ☐
- Move to new location ☐
- Draw against commission after 90 days ☐

Your personal cons from the job:

____

____

____

____

____

____

____

____

____

Sample deal breakers/killers (from the cons)

Possible future relocation

45-minute commute each way

YOUR ANALYSIS OF JOB OFFER

SAMPLE CONCLUSION

90-minute daily commute and extensive travel using personal car make it a no-go at any salary!

OR . . .

Salary good but politically not aligned with me. Noted antimilitary attitude.

OR . . .

GREAT opportunity in home town. Starting salary adequate with potential for bonuses and raises.

YOUR CONCLUSION =

CLOSING THOUGHTS

I'm glad you chose TheHireTactics™ to learn a proven method of conducting a strategic job search instead of relying on an outdated, traditional job search everyone uses that is clearly no longer effective in today's new economy.

Greg Wood and I have provided you with a lot of very valuable information, including the tools and resources that you need to conduct a successful search. Now it's up to you to mix and match them to best fit your needs. As you do this, make sure you customize your approach so that everything you present to a potential hiring manager is a true reflection of who you are and the value you offer.

Remember your value as your career progresses, and continue to reinvent yourself. Understand what it is you offer the business community and learn to adjust to a global economy that can affect your employment at any time. It's important that, even while employed, you continue to build your professional network and explore other opportunities. Remember, you're a professional first and someone else's employee second.

You'll find TheHireTactics™ will continue to be a valuable resource as your career moves forward. The strategies we've introduced will provide you with the direction for success when you **again** find yourself in transition, and faced with the key challenge of **differentiation.**

As a fellow veteran I continue to wish you the very best and thank you for serving your country.

Limits of Liability and Disclaimers of Warranties
Results, Earnings and Income Disclaimers

The material in this book is provided as is and without any kind of express or implied warranties. We make no guarantees that you will achieve any results from applying the author's ideas, strategies, and tactics found in this book. Because the book is a general educational information product, it is not a substitute for professional advice on the topics presented or discussed herein.

The author does not warrant or make any representations regarding the use or the results of the use of the materials in this book in terms of their correctness, accuracy, reliability, or otherwise. We make no earnings projections, promises, or representations of any kind.

The author and the publisher do not warrant this book is free from defects or that any such defects will be corrected. We further do not assume liability for nor warrant or guarantee websites, devices, or other delivery systems related to this book are free from viruses or other malware.

The author and the publisher assume no responsibility for any losses or damages resulting from your use of any link, information, or opportunity contained in this book or within any other information disclosed by the author or the publisher in any form whatsoever.

You agree to hold the author and the publisher of this book, principals, agents, affiliates, associates, and employees harmless from any and all liability for all claims for damages, including attorney's fees and costs, incurred by you or caused to third parties by you, arising out of the use or application of products, services, and activities discussed in this book. Further, the author and/or publisher are not liable for any damages that result from the use or the inability to use the information in this book even if the author, the publisher or an authorized representative has been made aware of the possibility of such damages. Should compensation be awarded for damages, losses, and causes of action (whether contract or tort including but not limited to negligence), the total awards, penalties, and costs shall not exceed the amount paid by you, if any, for this book.

You are advised to perform your own due diligence when it comes to making any decisions on materials provided in this book. Use caution and seek the advice of qualified professional before acting upon the contents of this book or any other information. You shall not consider any examples, documents, or other content of this book or otherwise provided by the author or publisher to be the equivalent of professional advice.

You should always conduct your own investigation (perform due diligence) before implementing strategies and tactics mentioned in this book or buying products or services from anyone, be it offline or via the Internet, including products and services sold via hyperlinks embedded in this book.

Due Diligence

You are advised to perform your own due diligence when it comes to making any decisions. Use caution and seek the advice of qualified professional before acting upon the contents of this book or any other information related to its use. You shall not consider any explanations, presentations, examples, documents, or other content in this book or otherwise provided by the author or publisher using means such as but not limited to webinars or conferences, to be the equivalent of professional advice.

The author and the publisher assume no responsibility for any losses or damages resulting from your use of any link, information, or opportunity contained in this book or within any other information disclosed by the author or the publisher in any form whatsoever.

Affiliate Compensation & Connections Disclosure

Any recommended products or services mentioned in this book are based on the author's belief that the purchase of such products and services will help the readers in general or specific to the topic of this book. However, the reader is assumed to have performed their own due diligence prior to making any such purchases of a product or service mentioned in this book.

This book contains hyperlinks to websites and information created and maintained by other individuals and organizations (third parties) in addition to those owned or operated by the author and/or the publisher. The author and the publisher do not control or guarantee the accuracy, relevance, or timeliness of any information or privacy policies posted on these outside, third-party websites.

Some third parties may have a material connection to the author and/or publisher. Such third parties to hereafter be known individually and collectively as the affiliate. Because of the potential for a material connection, the reader is to always assume that the author and/or publisher may be biased because of the affiliate's relationship with the author and/or publisher and/or because the affiliate has offered or will provide something of value or compensation.

The type of compensation received by the affiliate will vary. In some instances the affiliate may provide products or services for review or use or may provide other compensation. The affiliate may further provide monetary or nonmonetary compensation to the author and/or publisher when you take an action by clicking a hyperlink in this book or make a purchase.

Purchase Price

Although the publisher believes the price is fair for the value you receive, you understand and agree the purchase price for this book has been arbitrarily set by the publisher and has no relationship to value, guarantees, or objective standards.

THEHIREROAD™ JOB SEARCH SYSTEM

We know some of you may need more help than just this book. We also know you may not have access to the resources you need if you are deployed or live in an area without nearby access to VA resources. So if you are serious about changing your mindset and implementing the tactics we've described in this book then TheHireRoad™ job-search tutorial may be your answer.

In addition to showing you how to prepare the critical new tool of a biography, the program introduces other innovative tactics and strategies such as management endorsements, the post-interview packet, and the 90+ question audio interview CD, all to help you stand head and shoulders above your competition!

Learn the language of the civilian job search protocols and rehearse them. Get templates and samples of biographies and the necessary professionally-written resumes and cover letters.

To learn more visit http://www.TheHireChallenge.com.

APPENDIX

Glossary

Job hunting has its own language. Here are some of the terms you may hear in your job search:

Fiduciary Responsibility—The legal requirement that a company and its management first meet the needs of investors for profitability of their bonds and stocks. That means if a company can make more money for the stockholders by downsizing or outsourcing, they have a legal obligation to consider doing so. Employers generally have NO fiduciary responsibility to their employees to maintain their jobs other than contractual requirements. This is why companies do NOT want to hire employees.

Hiring Manager—An individual who will actually be in your chain of command. These are the employees such as your direct supervisor or the department head. These are the individuals who actually KNOW what the job requirements must be and have the flexibility to recognize what skills and value you may bring to the position beyond bland and meaningless keywords. Your goal is interaction with the hiring manager, NOT human resources.

Keywords—Used for search engine optimization (SEO) and sorting through large amounts of data. Keywords are used to find information on the internet and many career sites require you to select one or more keywords to search for jobs. Many sites also ask you to provide your own keywords as part of uploading your resume.

Keywords for job searches are words that describe a job, skills, or qualification. For example, "engineering" or "hospitality" are single critical keywords that describe a job or skill as well as industry. Single critical keywords are usually combined into longtail keyword phrases like "oil field engineering" or "casino and gaming hospitality." Failure to have these keywords and phrases in your resume means you will be rejected by any organization using an online screening program.

Meatgrinder—A computer program that scans resumes and applications for keywords and phrases. The bigger the company the more likely they are to require you to complete the application online and/or upload your resume to a website for review. Your materials will then be reviewed by a computer program or by an outside HR service that has been told what keywords and phrases best represent what the employer is looking for.

Social Media—Online chat and connection sites. For job applicants, LinkedIn is the recognized leader in job searches. However, do not overlook reaching out using sites like Goggle+, Facebook, Twitter, and specialty sites for your industry. Equally, make sure you have removed anything questionable from your site—both your postings and friends—that may reflect badly on you should a prospective employer do a Google search on you as part of the hiring process.

NOTES

NOTES

NOTES

NOTES

NOTES

NOTES

NOTES

NOTES